White Elephant
Book for Adults

All rights are reserved 2024 by Life Style Daily. No part of this publication may be reproduced, stored in a retrieval system or transmitted in any form or by any means, electronic, mechanical, photocopying, recording or otherwise, without prior permission.

Table Of Contents

Table Of Contents 2

Chapter 1.1: The History and Origins of the White Elephant Game 4

Chapter 1.2: Why White Elephant Is So Popular 6

Chapter 1.3: Dirty Santa vs. White Elephant – Differences and Similarities 8

Chapter 2.1: Planning the Party 11

Chapter 2.2: Setting the Gift Budget 14

Chapter 2.3: Decorations and Party Theme 17

Chapter 3.1: Basic Rules of White Elephant 20

Chapter 3.2: Extended Variants: Rule Modifications 23

Chapter 3.2: Extended Variants: Rule Modifications 26

Chapter 3.3: How to Choose the Right Variant for Your Group 28

Chapter 4.1: Classic and Universal Gifts 31

Chapter 4.2: DIY Gifts 34

Chapter 4.3: Gifts for Adults 36

Chapter 4.4: Themed Gifts 39

Chapter 5.1: Accompanying Mini-Games 42

Chapter 5.2: Challenges and Tasks for Participants 46

Chapter 5.3: Holiday Quiz Question Set 50

Chapter 6.2: Worst Gifts and Biggest Flops 53

Chapter 6.3: Most Surprising Gifts 57

Chapter 7.1: Funny Stories and Anecdotes from Gift Exchanges 60

Chapter 7.2: The Most Memorable White Elephant Gifts 63

Chapter 7.3: Blunders That Teach (and Amuse) 66
Chapter 8.1: White Elephant Game Cards 69
Chapter 8.2: White Elephant Wish List Templates 72
Chapter 8.3: Task Coupons for White Elephant Drawings 76
Chapter 9.1: Humorous Holiday Wishes 80
Chapter 9.2: Humorous Quotes About Gifts and the Holidays 82
Chapter 9.3: Wishes to Make Guests Laugh..85
Chapter 10.1: Tips for Future Holiday Gatherings 88
Chapter 10.2: How to Choose the Perfect White Elephant Gift.............91
Chapter 10.3: Preparing for Surprises and Challenges.........................93
Summary: White Elephant Book for Adults 96

3

Chapter 1.1: The History and Origins of the White Elephant Game

The White Elephant game has a deeper meaning than may appear at first glance. While the modern version is all about exchanging funny gifts for entertainment, the game's roots go back to a time when gifts held much more serious significance. Understanding the origins and evolution of White Elephant helps capture the spirit of the game and why it remains popular to this day.

1. The Legend of the White Elephant

The legend of the white elephant originates from Asia, particularly in regions like Thailand, Myanmar (Burma), and India, where these rare animals were considered royal and sacred symbols. White elephants, extremely rare and highly valued, were often regarded as signs of wealth, prosperity, and good fortune. Occasionally, rulers would gift white elephants to other nobles to show respect or strengthen political alliances. Although receiving such a gift was a great honor, it was also a challenge—white elephants required special care and couldn't be used for work, meaning significant expenses came with their upkeep. Over time, the term "white elephant gift" began to refer to presents that, while beautiful, were inconvenient or costly to own.

This symbolism endures in the White Elephant game, where participants exchange gifts of unexpected value. Today, however, the game is purely humorous—a lighthearted activity rather than a burdensome commitment.

2. The Emergence of the Modern Game

The modern version of White Elephant appeared in the United States around the 20th century, as holiday gatherings and gift exchanges grew more popular. As new generations moved away from formal gift-giving traditions, alternative ways of exchanging gifts evolved to focus mainly on fun.

Initially, White Elephant didn't include any rules around "stealing" gifts; participants simply exchanged presents in a set order, opening each one without competition. This relaxed version provided a low-key alternative to formal gift exchanges. Later, the "steal" rule was introduced, adding a competitive element that made White Elephant more engaging.

3. The Evolution of Rules and Popularization

The introduction of the "steal" rule brought a whole new dynamic to the game—participants could now choose between opening a new gift or taking one that someone else had already opened. Each "steal" adds excitement and energy, especially as people begin competing for the most coveted gifts. Over time, different versions of the game emerged, adapted to local customs and senses of humor, which contributed to its growing popularity.

By the 1980s and 90s, White Elephant became popular at office holiday parties, where employees enjoyed the fun, relaxed atmosphere of the game. People began creating their own rules, like limiting the number of steals or allowing a gift to be "bought back." As a result, White Elephant spread to family and friends' gatherings, gaining popularity as a holiday game that was easy to organize and offered lots of laughs and memorable moments.

4. Game Variants Around the World

Over the years, White Elephant spread to different regions, adopting local names and variations. In the southern United States, it became known as "Dirty Santa," hinting at a more mischievous and playful style. In the northern states and Canada, there's also a variant called "Yankee Swap." Each version has a slightly different flavor and its own unique rules.

Dirty Santa sometimes involves a more provocative or humorous approach, while Yankee Swap tends to be a bit more restrained, allowing for more customizable rules. These variations show how games like White Elephant adapt to the style and culture of different groups.

5. Why White Elephant Remains Popular

White Elephant has endured as one of the most popular holiday games because it combines elements of humor, competition, and surprise. The game encourages participants to interact and laugh together, making every gift exchange a unique and lively event. It's a lighthearted way to exchange gifts, often with items that range from clever to completely absurd.

The game is fitting for various gatherings, not only holiday events. Its flexibility and adaptability allow it to suit different occasions, and the number of participants can easily be adjusted. This versatility has kept White Elephant as a game that brings laughter and unforgettable moments, no matter who's playing.

6. Summary

White Elephant is a game that has stood the test of time, adapting to different cultures and evolving its rules to entertain as many people as possible. Whether it's a formal office gift exchange or a relaxed gathering with friends, White Elephant brings joy and laughter. It's more than just a game—it's an opportunity to spend time with loved ones, share in humor, and create memories that will be cherished for years.

Chapter 1.2: Why White Elephant Is So Popular

White Elephant has gained popularity worldwide, particularly in the United States, due to its unique blend of humor, excitement, and social bonding. This popularity isn't accidental—the game meets the need for entertainment that is both uncomplicated and adaptable, allowing everyone to join in, regardless of age or interests. Let's explore a few key reasons why White Elephant has earned its nearly iconic status as a fun, festive way to celebrate together.

1. Ease of Organization and Simple Rules

One of the main reasons for White Elephant's popularity is its simplicity. No elaborate preparations or special supplies are needed—just a group of people, a few gifts, and clear rules. White Elephant doesn't require any special skills from the organizer or participants, making it an ideal choice for all kinds of gatherings. Whether for an office holiday party or a gathering of friends, a few basic guidelines are all that's needed for everyone to join in and enjoy the game.

This simplicity makes White Elephant a popular choice for companies and groups looking to avoid complicated logistics and planning. It works equally well for large gatherings with dozens of people or small, intimate home parties.

2. Laughter and Lightheartedness: Holiday Humor at Its Best

White Elephant is one of the few games that can make almost everyone laugh. The entire concept of exchanging "unusual" gifts encourages participants to approach it with humor and ease. Gifts can be funny, absurd, or even a little cheeky, sparking laughter and creating an atmosphere full of joy. White Elephant breaks through the traditional, often formal holiday mood by bringing in lighthearted energy that helps everyone feel more relaxed.

This playful approach to gifts lets people enjoy not only what they receive but also the reactions of others. This makes the game more interactive and engaging than a typical gift exchange, where each person simply receives a gift without much suspense or surprise.

3. The Element of Competition: "Stealing" Gifts

White Elephant introduces friendly competition with the "steal" rule. Participants can choose whether to open a new gift or take one that someone else already has. This game dynamic adds unpredictability, making each round suspenseful and lively. Any gift can change hands several times, increasing the excitement and laughter, especially when there's a battle over the most desired or funniest item.

The "steal" feature makes White Elephant perfect for group gatherings, as it involves everyone, whether they're opening a gift or just watching the action. Each person gets a moment to make a bold move and maybe become the hero of the moment, adding a fun blend of excitement and laughter to the game.

4. Bonding and Community Building

White Elephant fosters bonding and strengthens connections among participants. Through shared fun and laughter, the game serves as a fantastic way to build positive relationships, whether among friends or coworkers. With its relaxed, playful gift exchange, it encourages participants to get to know each other better, chat about the chosen gifts, and share reactions.

At office holiday parties, White Elephant is a great way to break down formal barriers and build relationships in a friendly, informal setting. In family or friend gatherings, the game reminds everyone of the joy of spending time together and appreciating each others presence.

5. Flexibility and Customization

White Elephant is a flexible game, meaning it can easily be adapted for any group or occasion. There are many variations of the game, from more reserved versions to cheekier ones, allowing it to suit the group's needs. Among friends, where humor may be more relaxed, gifts can be bolder. In an office setting, where the game is more formal, gifts may be funny but neutral.

This flexibility also means that White Elephant isn't limited to just the holidays. It can be played at any party, such as birthdays, anniversaries, or themed gatherings. Any occasion can be a great reason to host a White Elephant game, with rules easily customized to fit the gathering's style.

6. White Elephant as an Alternative to Holiday Consumerism

Many people find themselves turned off by the holiday season's consumerism, which often overshadows the true meaning of the holidays. White Elephant offers a refreshing alternative—focusing more on humor and togetherness than on the material value of gifts. This approach makes White Elephant a symbol of a return to simple joys and a reminder that the real value lies in time spent with loved ones.

White Elephant, then, is an alternative to expensive gifts and offers participants a chance to celebrate without pressure. People can choose gifts that are funny, unusual, or entirely worthless in a material sense, allowing everyone to avoid spending a lot of money. This makes White Elephant a game that fits well with today's desire for authentic, non-commercial ways to celebrate.

Summary

White Elephant's popularity stems from its flexibility, humor, and easy organization. Its rules allow participants to enjoy, laugh, and connect, creating lasting memories. White Elephant combines elements of competition, humor, and social bonding, making it the perfect game for the holiday spirit.

White Elephant remains one of the most popular holiday games, drawing people of all ages and backgrounds. Whether played with family, friends, or coworkers, White Elephant is a game that brings plenty of joy and laughter, making each gathering memorable.

Chapter 1.3: Dirty Santa vs. White Elephant – Differences and Similarities

While the games White Elephant and Dirty Santa are often used interchangeably and share similar rules, there are subtle differences between them. In both games, the main goal is entertainment through the exchange of humorous, quirky gifts, but the way these gifts are presented and traded can vary depending on the version. Let's take a closer look at the differences and similarities between these two games to better understand which one might be the right choice for your gathering.

1. Similarities Between Dirty Santa and White Elephant

Both games share common rules and objectives: to bring joy and bonding among participants through a fun gift exchange. In both versions, participants draw or choose gifts in a way that adds unpredictability and humor to the game. Here are the key similarities:

Game Mechanics: In both versions, participants have the option to either open a new gift or "steal" one from another player. This rule introduces a level of competition that often leads to laughter as popular gifts change hands repeatedly.

Funny and Unusual Gifts: The central appeal in both Dirty Santa and White Elephant is in the funny, quirky, or completely impractical gifts. The goal is to spread joy with offbeat gifts that aren't necessarily valuable but are chosen for entertainment.

Participant Interaction: Both games are excellent icebreakers, creating a relaxed and enjoyable atmosphere. The "steal" rule brings a shared sense of playfulness and friendly competition.

Occasions: While most commonly played at holiday gatherings, both Dirty Santa and White Elephant can be enjoyed at other events, like birthdays, anniversaries, or office parties.

2. Differences Between Dirty Santa and White Elephant

Despite their similarities, certain distinctions arise from regional differences and various interpretations of the games. Knowing these differences can help match the game's style to the gathering's tone and participant preferences.

Name and Regional Context: Dirty Santa is most popular in the southern United States, while White Elephant is widely recognized across the country and even beyond. This distinction can influence participants' perceptions—"Dirty Santa" suggests a more mischievous and playful vibe, while "White Elephant" is a bit more neutral.

Type of Gifts: In Dirty Santa, gifts may be more "daring" or a bit cheeky, making it better suited to parties where participants are open to funny or sometimes provocative presents. In contrast, White Elephant gifts are generally less bold and more neutral, making this version appropriate for more diverse groups, such as family gatherings or workplace events.

Level of Mischievousness: Dirty Santa encourages gifts that might surprise or amuse participants in a more playful way than White Elephant. For example, a Dirty Santa gift might include a humorous figurine or an odd gadget that references private jokes within the group. White Elephant focuses on humorous gifts but typically less provocative ones.

3. When to Choose Dirty Santa vs. White Elephant

Choosing between Dirty Santa and White Elephant depends largely on the nature of the gathering and the relationships between participants. Here are some tips to help decide:

Family or Formal Gatherings: In these settings, White Elephant is usually a better choice, as it's more neutral and universally appropriate. The gifts can be funny without crossing boundaries of good taste, helping to avoid potential misunderstandings.

Parties with Friends or Informal Groups: Dirty Santa is a more fitting option for gatherings where participants know each other well and share a similar sense of humor. This version of the game allows for cheekier gifts that reference shared experiences or inside jokes.

Work Gatherings: In a workplace context, White Elephant is generally a safer choice since the rules and gifts can be more easily tailored to a formal atmosphere. Dirty Santa can be fun but may require closer oversight of gift selection to avoid any potentially awkward situations.

4. Customizing the Game for Your Group

For many organizers, blending elements of both games can be the best approach. You can adopt the general rules of White Elephant while adding playful elements from Dirty Santa, like task cards or humorous challenges for participants to draw during the game. This approach provides flexibility, allowing participants to enjoy the game in their own way without being limited to one version.

5. Summary: Which Version of the Game is Right for Your Event?

Dirty Santa and White Elephant are both centered around the shared experience of exchanging gifts and having fun. Choosing between them depends on the tone of the gathering and the participants' expectations. If you're looking for a more neutral and lighthearted atmosphere, White Elephant is the safer choice. For those seeking a bit more mischievous, spirited fun, Dirty Santa is the ideal pick. In either case, the most important thing is for participants to enjoy the moment and play in the spirit of holiday cheer.

Chapter 2.1: Planning the Party

Planning a White Elephant party might seem simple, but careful organization ensures the event goes smoothly and is full of laughter and positive vibes. In this section, we'll cover steps to help you plan the party from start to finish so that everyone—both guests and the host—can enjoy their time together.

1. Setting the Date and Time

One of the first steps is selecting a date and time for the gathering. Here are a few tips for planning a White Elephant party:

Holiday Season: White Elephant parties are most commonly held around the holiday season, especially before Christmas. Choose a date that allows guests to attend comfortably, ideally a few days before the holiday.

Time: Evenings are ideal for these gatherings, as they allow guests to fully relax and engage without time pressure. Pick a time that works for most guests, considering their schedules, such as an evening after work or a weekend afternoon.

Coordinating with Other Events: If you're organizing a company party or a gathering among friends, check to ensure the date doesn't clash with other events. For larger groups, it can be helpful to send out a poll or ask for availability to let everyone share their preferred time.

2. Guest List and Group Size

The next step is creating a guest list and deciding on the number of participants. Choosing the right number is key to ensuring the game is engaging and enjoyable:

Small Groups (up to 10 people): Perfect for more intimate gatherings, like family or close friends. In smaller groups, participants can get to know each other better, and the atmosphere is cozier.

Medium Groups (10–20 people): Great for company events or larger friend gatherings. More participants add energy to the game as gifts change hands more frequently.

Large Groups (over 20 people): White Elephant can be organized for even larger groups, such as company parties. For these, consider adding extra rules to speed up the game or make gift exchanges easier.

Consider how well guests know each other. If participants are strangers, a brief introduction can help everyone feel more at ease and comfortable.

3. Choosing a Party Theme

Though White Elephant is traditionally associated with the holiday season, adding a theme can make it unique and allow guests to get even more creative:

Holiday Atmosphere: Classic holiday decorations like a tree, lights, and festive tablecloths create a seasonal feel and put guests in a holiday mood.

Themed Parties: White Elephant can work with any theme, such as "Retro" (80s or 90s), "Hollywood," "Movie Heroes," or "Wild Animals." Each theme can inspire gift selections and decorations.

Dress Code: Introduce a themed dress code, like funny holiday sweaters, colorful outfits, or costumes, to add humor and immerse guests further into the party's vibe.

4. Preparing the Space and Decorations

Setting up the venue is essential for creating a comfortable and enjoyable atmosphere. Here are some tips for organizing the ideal space for a White Elephant party:

Gift Exchange Area: Arrange seating in a circle or semicircle to allow for easy gift exchanges and for guests to watch each others reactions. This area can be decorated with holiday ornaments or elements that fit the theme.

Snack and Drink Table: Every party needs food and drinks to help guests feel comfortable and give them a chance to chat outside the game. Choose easy-to-eat snacks, like sandwiches, mini pizzas, skewers, and both non-alcoholic and alcoholic beverages if appropriate for the group.

Decorations: Decorations depend on the theme but consider colorful lights, garlands, and balloons. Holiday elements like a Christmas tree can add to the festive feel.

5. Preparing Game Instructions and Rules

It's a good idea to prepare a short set of instructions to explain at the beginning of the game. Here are a few tips for effectively explaining the rules:

Rule Reminder: Even if most participants know the rules, a quick reminder is helpful. Explain how the gift exchange works, the options for "stealing" gifts, and any limits on the number of times a gift can change hands.

Special Rules: If you have additional rules, such as a "steal" limit or the option to draw tasks, explain them briefly at the start to avoid confusion.

Rule Cards: Preparing small cards with key rules or a list of gifts can be useful, especially for larger parties. Guests can refer to them if they have questions.

6. Invitations and RSVP

Sending invitations is an important part of planning, helping to ensure everyone is informed about the event and its details. Here are some ways to effectively invite guests:

Choosing an Invitation Method: You can send traditional paper invitations for an elegant touch or use online invitations, which are quick and convenient. Email invites or social media messages make it easy to communicate and send reminders.

Details in the Invitation: Make sure the invitation includes the date, time, location, dress code, theme, and game rules. It's also helpful to provide guidelines on the value or nature of gifts so that participants know how to prepare.

RSVP: Request RSVP s in the invitation to plan seating, snacks, and the number of gifts accordingly.

7. Planning a Party Timeline

Creating a general timeline helps the party flow smoothly and stay on track. Here are a few sample steps to consider:

Welcoming Guests: Spend the first few minutes greeting guests, who can grab snacks before the game begins.

Starting the White Elephant Game: Once most guests have arrived, begin the game by explaining the rules and organizing participants.

Gift Exchange: Depending on the number of people, the game may last from 30 minutes to an hour or more. Make sure everyone has a chance to participate and feels included.

Closing and Social Time: After the game, allow time for guests to relax, chat, and share impressions. You can also include a few mini-games if time allows.

Summary

Planning a White Elephant party involves many elements—from selecting a date and guest list to setting up the space and decorations. Each detail contributes to the atmosphere and comfort of participants. With thoughtful planning, the game will run smoothly, and your guests will remember the gathering with a smile.

Chapter 2.2: Setting the Gift Budget

Setting a budget for gifts is one of the most important aspects of organizing a White Elephant party. Establishing a price range in advance allows participants to select suitable gifts and ensures everyone feels comfortable knowing how much to spend. A well-chosen budget enhances the enjoyment of the game and eliminates potential misunderstandings.

1. Why Is a Budget Important?

The gift budget plays a key role in balancing the game. Here are a few reasons why setting a price range is beneficial:

Consistency in Gifts: When everyone knows the spending limit, gifts are generally of similar value, preventing anyone from feeling disappointed or left out.

Participant Convenience: A clear budget allows participants to choose their gifts without wondering if their contribution is "good enough," reducing stress and increasing satisfaction.

Cost Control: An established budget helps avoid overspending and ensures the event is both enjoyable and financially accessible for everyone.

2. How to Choose the Right Budget

The gift budget for White Elephant should be tailored to the group's makeup and the nature of the gathering. Here are some factors to consider when selecting a budget:

Nature of the Event: At company gatherings or large parties, the budget can vary—ranging from modest to slightly higher-end gifts. In a family or close friends setting, a lower budget is common, allowing everyone to join in without feeling pressured to spend a lot.

Participant Preferences: It's helpful to check with participants or take a quick poll to see what price range feels comfortable for them. If the group is financially diverse, a lower budget is generally better.

Suggested Price Ranges:

$10–$15: Great for fun trinkets, novelty items, and small DIY gifts.

$15–$25: The most commonly chosen range, offering a mix of practical and humorous gifts.

$25–$50: Ideal for more formal events or company gatherings, allowing for higher-quality gifts.

Maximum Value: In some groups, setting a maximum amount rather than a range, like "up to $20," gives more flexibility in gift selection.

3. Creative Gift Ideas by Budget

Each group can benefit from inspiration for gifts that fit within the set budget. Here are some suggestions by price range:

$10–$15 Budget:

- Funny mugs with witty phrases
- Socks with quirky designs
- Mini tabletop games (like mini dominoes)
- Notebooks with humorous covers

$15–$25 Budget:

- Holiday-themed candy sets
- Thermal mugs or travel mugs
- Scented candles in holiday packaging

- Card games like Uno or Cards Against Humanity

$25–$50 Budget:

- Coffee or tea gift sets

- Holiday decorations or ornament sets

- Wine accessories, like corkscrews or glasses

- Board games for social gatherings

A set budget doesn't have to limit creativity—the main goal is for gifts to be funny and either humorous or practical, ensuring everyone finds something they enjoy.

4. DIY Gifts: Save Money and Add a Personal Touch

DIY (Do It Yourself) gifts are a fantastic way to save money while adding a personal touch to the present. Handmade gifts can be just as fun and appreciated as purchased ones, while also being unique. Here are a few DIY gift ideas that fit within a low budget:

Homemade Hot Chocolate Kit: Fill small jars with hot chocolate mix, add marshmallows, and tie with a ribbon.

Challenge Jar: Fill a jar with fun challenges, like "Say something nice about the person to your right"—perfect for social gatherings.

Mini Snack Basket: Arrange a small basket with assorted treats, nuts, and snacks—a small but tasty gift.

5. Communicating the Budget in Invitations

Be clear about the gift budget in the invitations so that each participant knows the appropriate price range. Here are a few ways to effectively communicate the budget:

Note in the Invitation: Include a line like, "Please bring a gift within the $15–$25 range so everyone has a fair chance to receive something fun!"

Playful Suggestion: Try writing, "The gift budget is $20—let's see who can find the funniest present within that limit!" This can set a lighthearted tone and encourage creativity.

Verbal Reminder: For smaller, more intimate gatherings, simply mention the budget in person or via text.

6. Establishing Budget Rules

If the group is diverse, consider setting a few extra guidelines related to the budget:

Maximum Limit: Setting a maximum amount, such as "up to $30," gives everyone the freedom to choose while maintaining balance.

No Additional Extras: Set the rule that the gift should only include what fits the budget, avoiding extra items that might exceed it.

Budget Confirmation: If participants are unsure about the gift's value, they can check with the organizer, especially if they plan to add something extra.

Summary

Setting a budget for gifts is a crucial step that affects the comfort and satisfaction of participants. Clear guidelines on gift values help avoid misunderstandings and create a friendly, fair atmosphere. With the right budget, everyone can enjoy fun, unique gifts that are a perfect addition to the holiday celebration.

Chapter 2.3: Decorations and Party Theme

One of the key elements of a White Elephant party, aside from the game itself, is creating the right atmosphere with decorations and a chosen theme. Well-chosen decorations set the festive and playful tone, while a specific theme allows for added creativity. In this chapter, we'll look at theme inspirations, decoration ideas, and tips for creating a unique party vibe.

1. Choosing a Party Theme

Defining a theme is the first step to giving the party its own unique flair. A classic holiday theme works well, but if you want your event to stand out, try a specific motif. Here are some ideas for White Elephant party themes:

Classic Holiday Atmosphere: A Christmas tree, lights, red-and-green decorations, and holiday music make for a timeless, universally appealing setting. Perfect for family and office gatherings where everyone enjoys the familiar holiday spirit.

Ugly Sweater Party: Each guest wears their ugliest, most over-the-top holiday sweater, adding a humorous twist to the event. This theme works great with casual groups where everyone can have a laugh at themselves.

Winter Wonderland: Snow-inspired decorations—fake snow, white and silver accents, mini trees, and cool-toned lights—create an elegant theme. Ideal for more formal gatherings where subtlety and beauty matter.

Retro Christmas: Decorate in a style inspired by past decades—like the 50s, 60s, or 80s—with vintage ornaments and music. Classic baubles, retro decor, and holiday songs from those eras add a nostalgic, cozy feel.

Tropical Christmas: For a warm twist on winter, go tropical with palm trees, flamingos, pink, turquoise, and green hues, and exotic cocktails. A fun way to make the White Elephant party unique and memorable.

2. Decoration Ideas

Decorations should reflect the theme, creating a cohesive atmosphere that immerses guests as soon as they arrive. Here are a few decoration ideas to match different themes:

Holiday Lights: String lights in warm white or colorful garlands add charm to any gathering. Hang them around windows, furniture, or even around the gift exchange area.

Garlands and Banners: Holiday garlands or those in specific color schemes (like white, red, or green) can create a focal point. Banners with playful phrases like "White Elephant," "Merry & Bright," or "Let the Stealing Begin" add humor and fit the party theme.

Table Decorations: On the snack and drink table, use holiday-themed tablecloths and add small decorations like pinecones, fir branches, mini ornaments, or candles. Theme-specific accents, like tropical flowers for "Tropical Christmas" or red-and-green touches for "Classic Holiday," keep the decor consistent.

Figurines and Festive Decor: Small figurines of reindeer, trees, Santa, or even fake snow enhance the holiday atmosphere. Scatter them around the room for extra festive touches.

3. Extra Touches and Attractions

Adding themed extras and activities allows guests to dive deeper into the atmosphere and makes the party unique:

Themed Photo Booth: Set up a small area with a decorative backdrop where guests can take photos. Include fun props like Santa hats, reindeer antlers, festive glasses, or signs with phrases like "Ho Ho Ho" and "Let It Snow." A photo booth adds extra fun and a memorable keepsake.

Themed Stickers and Gift Tags: Each gift can be labeled with stickers or tags that match the theme. Stickers with reindeer, trees, or palm trees depending on the theme not only add a decorative touch but also help differentiate the gifts and give them character.

Holiday Music: Music is essential for setting the party's backdrop. Create a playlist with classic holiday songs or, if the party has a tropical or retro theme, add music that matches that vibe. You can even include humorous versions of popular holiday tunes.

Festive Drinks and Beverages: Offer drinks that suit the theme, like mulled wine, hot chocolate, or cocktails with cinnamon, ginger, or citrus for a holiday feel. For "Tropical Christmas," serve drinks with umbrellas and slices of exotic fruit.

4. Organizing the Gift Exchange Area

The main event is the gift exchange area, so plan the space with enough room for participants to sit comfortably and watch the gift trading.

Seating Arrangement: Arrange seats in a circle or semicircle so everyone has a clear view of the other guests and the gifts. This setup allows everyone to see reactions to "steals" and trades.

Gift Area: Place a table or shelf in a central spot for the gifts. This makes it easy to pick out gifts and lets each package be displayed. Decorate the table with holiday accents like lights or small Christmas trees.

Game Rules Sign: For large gatherings or groups with new players, it's helpful to have a small sign or card with the game rules. This adds a practical and decorative element to the setup.

5. Adding Personal Touches to Decorations

Personalizing the decorations makes guests feel special and shows your attention to detail:

Customized Drink Labels: Create labels for drinks with guests' names or funny phrases to add a personal touch to the party.

Mini Thank-You Gifts for Guests: Small treats or holiday-themed goodies can be given to each guest as a thank-you for attending. These could be simple, like chocolates in holiday bags tied with ribbon.

Summary

Decorations and the party theme play a crucial role in setting the mood for a White Elephant event. Choosing the right theme, matching the decorations, and adding special touches like a photo booth or themed drinks ensure that guests feel part of a unique celebration. With thoughtful planning, your party will be a memorable event filled with laughter, holiday spirit, and positive energy.

Chapter 3.1: Basic Rules of White Elephant

White Elephant is a game designed for fun and group bonding, where participants exchange gifts in a relaxed, playful atmosphere. The rules are simple, and the element of "stealing" gifts brings a level of unpredictability, adding excitement and laughter. In this section, we'll go through the basic rules of White Elephant, which can be adjusted for any group, whether family, friends, or coworkers.

1. Preparing for the Game

White Elephant begins by gathering the right number of gifts. Each participant brings one wrapped gift, which should fit within a pre-set budget. Gifts should be anonymous and wrapped in a way that conceals their contents—the more mysterious, the better!

Number of Gifts: Each player brings one gift, so there is an equal number of participants and gifts. For example, if there are 10 players, there should be 10 gifts.

Wrapping: Gifts should be wrapped to keep their contents a surprise. Mystery and anticipation are key to the fun!

2. Starting the Game and Choosing Order

Each participant draws a number to determine their order. This can be done by drawing numbers or pulling slips with numbers on them.

First Player: The person with number 1 chooses a gift from the pile and opens it in front of everyone so that everyone can see what they received.

Subsequent Players: The second player can either pick a new gift or "steal" an already opened gift from a previous player. If they choose to steal, the person whose gift was taken picks a new gift from the pile.

Continuing the Game: Each subsequent player follows this pattern—either picking a new gift or "stealing" an already opened one from another participant.

3. Rules for "Stealing" Gifts

The "stealing" aspect of White Elephant adds excitement and humor, as even the most popular gifts can change hands multiple times. Here are the key rules for gift "stealing":

Steal Limits: Often, there is a limit to how many times a gift can be "stolen." A common rule is that a gift can change hands a maximum of three times, to keep the game moving and prevent it from dragging on.

Limit on Steals per Player: Some groups add a rule that each player can only "steal" one gift per turn, which helps maintain the game's flow and prevents extended rounds.

No Immediate Retakes: In White Elephant, participants cannot immediately "steal back" a gift from the person who just took it. They must wait until their next turn or try to steal a different gift.

4. The Final Round

The final round wraps up the game in a fair way, giving participants one last chance to end up with their desired gift.

Last Chance to Steal: After the final turn (when all gifts are opened), the first player has the right to make one last "steal." They can exchange their gift with any participant, as long as the desired gift hasn't reached its steal limit.

Ending the Game: Once the final round is complete, the game ends, and participants keep the gifts they hold. Everyone can enjoy the gifts they received, whether practical, funny, or completely unexpected.

5. Etiquette and Good Manners

While White Elephant is a lighthearted game of humor and competition, it's good to follow some basic etiquette to ensure an enjoyable experience for everyone:

Stay Lighthearted: White Elephant is all about taking a light-hearted approach to gifts—the goal is not to win valuable items, but simply to have a good time.

Avoid Commenting on Gift Value: Refrain from making comments about the gifts' value out loud, as it might make someone feel bad about their choice. Everyone brings what they feel is suitable within the set budget.

Politeness During Steals: "Stealing" adds excitement, but remember to be courteous. If someone "steals" your desired gift, it's best to take it in stride with a smile.

6. Rule Modifications

Each group can adapt White Elephant rules to suit their preferences and needs. Here are a few example modifications:

Time Limit: For larger groups, set a time limit on each turn, such as 30 seconds, to keep the game moving.

Gift Drawing: Instead of selecting from a pile, all gifts can be placed in a central spot, and players can draw numbers that assign them to specific gifts. This reduces the emphasis on stealing while still allowing for fun exchanges.

Additional Challenges: For extra humor, add a twist by introducing challenge cards that players draw when choosing a gift. For example, "Sing a holiday song" or "Say three nice things about the person to your left."

Summary

The basic rules of White Elephant are simple, making it easy for any participant to join and quick to explain to newcomers. White Elephant's defining feature is its flexibility—rules can be adjusted based on the group size and event atmosphere, while the stealing element gives the game its unique flair. This game lets participants enjoy an unpredictable gift exchange full of laughter and positive energy, making every White Elephant party memorable.

Chapter 3.2: Extended Variants: Rule Modifications

White Elephant is a game that can easily be tailored to different groups and occasions, making it exceptionally flexible and universal. Rule modifications introduce new, fun elements that add excitement and dynamics to the game. Below are several popular extended variants that can make the classic White Elephant game even more interesting and unpredictable.

1. Time Limit for Choosing Gifts

Adding a time limit keeps the game moving and helps avoid prolonged decisions.

Rule: Each participant has a set amount of time (e.g., 30 seconds) to decide whether to choose a new gift or "steal" a gift from another player.

Benefits: Players must act quickly, adding excitement and unpredictability. A time limit is particularly helpful in larger groups, where the game can otherwise drag on.

Extra Twist: If a participant doesn't decide within the allotted time, they automatically receive a random gift or are assigned the closest one.

2. Challenge Cards for Extra Fun

Challenge cards add humor and interaction by requiring players to complete a fun task when selecting a gift.

Rule: When a player selects a new gift from the pile or "steals" a gift, they also draw a challenge card and must complete the task before their turn ends.

Sample Challenges:

- "Sing a line from a holiday song."

- "Tell the funniest holiday story that happened to you."

- "Make a holiday wish for the person to your left."

Benefits: Challenge cards add a humorous touch and help players get to know each other better, making this variant perfect for informal gatherings where participants feel at ease.

3. "Life Points" for Gifts

This variant limits the number of "steals" each gift can endure before it becomes "locked."

Rule: Each gift has a set number of "life points," such as three. After a gift has been "stolen" three times, it is "locked" and can no longer be taken by another participant.

Benefits: Limiting the number of "steals" prevents gifts from changing hands indefinitely and adds a strategic element where players must decide if a "steal" is truly worth it.

Extra Twist: Players can earn additional "life points" for their gifts by completing specific challenges, adding even more excitement and competition.

4. Secret Missions or Rewards for Certain Gifts

Secret missions or hidden rewards add an element of surprise, rewarding players who play strategically.

Rule: Some gifts include hidden "missions" or "rewards" in the form of notes inside the package, giving the recipient a special task or privilege.

Example Missions:

- "You may 'steal' one extra gift during your turn."

- "Swap your gift with any participant after the game ends."

Benefits: Secret missions introduce an additional layer of mystery and strategy, surprising participants with unexpected perks.

5. Double Trouble (Double Draw)

The Double Draw variant increases interaction by allowing each player to choose two gifts in a single turn.

Rule: Each player selects two gifts on their turn—one for themselves and one for another participant, who must accept it.

Benefits: Double Draw adds an extra layer of interaction, as players can "gift" others in a playful way, especially if the gift turns out to be something funny or impractical.

Extra Twist: Players can decide if they want to swap both gifts, adding yet another level of unpredictability.

6. Final Gift Exchange

This variant allows for an additional round of gift swapping after the game ends, giving participants a last chance to get their desired gift.

Rule: After the game concludes, all participants draw numbers or slips indicating who they must swap gifts with, regardless of what they currently hold.

Benefits: This adds one more round of excitement to close the game, as everyone wonders who they'll end up swapping with.

Extra Twist: Participants can also exchange gifts with the person seated to their left or right, further heightening the suspense.

7. Adding Themed "Mystery Gifts"

Mystery gifts are a few specially wrapped items prepared by the organizer and placed among the regular gifts. These can be funny, impractical, or completely surprising.

Rule: The organizer adds 1–2 "mystery gifts" to the pile. When a player chooses a mystery gift, they can either keep it or swap it with another participant, who cannot refuse.

Benefits: Mystery gifts introduce an element of risk and fun, as no one knows what's inside the uniquely wrapped package.

8. Points or Prizes for Best Reactions

This variant adds a mini-competition to reward players for their most entertaining responses to gifts.

Rule: The organizer awards "points" or small prizes for the funniest reactions, most amusing gift explanations, or best "steals." At the end, an extra prize goes to the person with the most points.

Benefits: Points and prizes motivate participants to engage actively, adding humor throughout the game. This variant is perfect for friendly gatherings where players can enjoy a lighthearted competition.

Summary

Extended White Elephant variants allow you to introduce unique rules that adapt the game to the group's personality and occasion. Whether you opt for "mystery gifts," challenge cards, double draws, or secret missions, each modification adds an extra layer of humor, competition, and mystery. These variations make White Elephant an even more enjoyable and engaging game that can be customized for any gathering.

Chapter 3.2: Extended Variants: Rule Modifications

Modifying the rules of White Elephant allows for extra elements of dynamism and humor. Below are three popular variants that can make the classic game even more thrilling: Speed Elephant, Double Trouble, and Dice Santa.

3.2.1 Speed Elephant – Fast Gift Exchanges

Speed Elephant is a version of the game that introduces a time limit for choosing and exchanging gifts, requiring participants to make quick decisions and pick up the pace.

Rule: Each participant has a set amount of time (e.g., 15–30 seconds) to choose a gift or decide to "steal" a gift from another player. The organizer keeps track of time, and if someone doesn't decide within the time limit, they automatically receive the nearest unopened gift.

Objective: Speed Elephant adds excitement by requiring quick decisions, which heightens suspense and energy.

Example Modifications:

Extra Time for a Challenge: If a player wants an extra 10 seconds, they must complete a fun task, like singing a snippet of a holiday song or telling a funny story.

Penalty for Time Exceeded: If a player fails to decide in time, they lose the chance to "steal" in that round.

Benefits: Speed Elephant is perfect for larger groups where the game can drag due to long decisions. The fast pace makes players act on instinct, adding unpredictability to the game.

3.2.2 Double Trouble – Double the Choice

Double Trouble is a variant that boosts interaction and competition by letting players choose two gifts during their turn.

Rule: Each player, when it's their turn, selects two gifts—one for themselves and another for any participant they choose. The recipient of the second gift must accept it, even if it's not something they would have chosen.

Objective: Double Trouble enhances player interaction, as participants get the chance to "gift" others something funny or surprising.

Example Modifications:

Option to Swap Both Gifts: Players may swap places with the person they gifted, adding an extra layer of strategy.

Prize for the Most "On-Target" Gift: At the end of the game, a prize is awarded for the most interesting or well-chosen gift, encouraging participants to choose mindfully.

Benefits: Double Trouble adds humor and allows participants to get to know each other better. It's a great option for friend gatherings where players can "pass along" gifts in a playful way.

3.2.3 Dice Santa – Gift Exchange with Dice

Dice Santa is a White Elephant variant where decisions to choose or steal a gift are determined by a roll of the dice, adding a layer of randomness that makes the game even more unpredictable and exciting.

Rule: Each player rolls a die before choosing a gift. The roll outcome determines their action, such as:

1 – Open a new gift.

2 – Swap gifts with the person on your left.

3 – Swap gifts with the person on your right.

4 – Hide a gift (the player selects one gift that can't be "stolen" until the next round).

5 – "Steal" a gift from any participant.

6 – Choose a gift and pass it to a person of your choice.

Objective: Dice Santa introduces randomness, forcing participants to adapt to unpredictable situations.

Example Modifications:

Two Dice: In an advanced version, players roll two dice, combining actions like "steal" from the person on your left or "protect" a chosen gift.

Tasks for High Rolls: If a player rolls the maximum, they must complete a fun task, like dancing or sharing a holiday anecdote, before taking their action.

Benefits: Dice Santa adds a dynamic, random element to the game, keeping participants on their toes. It's especially entertaining in large groups, where each turn brings new surprises.

Summary

These three extended variants—Speed Elephant, Double Trouble, and Dice Santa—allow participants to enjoy White Elephant in a whole new way. Speed Elephant adds pace and quick decision-making, Double Trouble brings humor and interaction, and Dice Santa introduces randomness, making each turn unpredictable. Each of these variants can be adapted to fit the group's character, offering a unique twist on the classic White Elephant game.

Chapter 3.3: How to Choose the Right Variant for Your Group

Choosing the right White Elephant variant for your group depends on several factors, including the number of participants, their preferences, and the type of atmosphere you want to create. Some game variants are better suited for formal gatherings, while others are ideal for casual get-together with friends. This chapter offers guidelines to help you select a game variant that best matches your group and event type.

1. Determine the Number of Participants

The number of players greatly affects which variant works best:

Small Groups (5–10 people): For smaller groups, choose variants that encourage more interaction, like Double Trouble or Dice Santa. These variants add extra choices and randomness, increasing surprise and humor.

Medium Groups (10–20 people): In medium-sized groups, variants that keep the game moving, such as Speed Elephant, work well. This variant enforces a time limit for decisions, ensuring a smooth flow and preventing the game from dragging on.

Large Groups (20+ people): For larger groups where time may be an issue, choose variants based on randomness, like Dice Santa. The dice element means participants don't need to spend much time deciding, which helps keep the game's pace up.

2. Consider the Atmosphere of the Gathering

The type of event and the mood you want to create play a big role in choosing a variant:

Formal and Corporate Events: For formal gatherings or office holiday parties, stick with variants that are simple and don't require excessive involvement in playful challenges. Speed Elephant is a good choice, as it adds energy without needing a lot of interaction beyond gift selection.

Family Gatherings and Close Friends: For gatherings with people who know each other well, more playful variants like Double Trouble or Dice Santa are ideal. These allow for greater interaction, bringing humor and deepening connections among participants.

Themed or Costume Parties: For events with a specific theme or costumes, variants with extra challenges, like Dice Santa with task-based dice rolls, can add even more fun to the party atmosphere.

3. Take into Account Participants' Preferences

Each group has its own preferences, so it's important to consider them when choosing a variant:

Groups that Enjoy Humor and Challenges: If your guests are open to fun and enjoy challenges, choose interactive variants like Double Trouble and Dice Santa. These allow participants to swap gifts in a playful way and complete funny tasks, adding an extra layer of entertainment.

Groups that Prefer Simplicity: If your guests prefer a straightforward, quick game, Speed Elephant is the best choice. Simple rules and a time limit make it easy to explain, and the fast pace keeps everyone engaged.

Mixed Groups: If your group has participants of different ages or varying levels of familiarity, choose a versatile variant that doesn't require too much interaction. Speed Elephant or Double Trouble work well, as they are dynamic but don't involve tasks that need deep involvement.

4. Match Variants to Available Game Time

The amount of time you have for the game is an important factor:

Limited Time: If the game is only one of many activities at the event, and time is tight, go with Speed Elephant. The time limit keeps the game from dragging on, so participants make quick decisions and move on to the next round.

No Time Constraints: If your gathering has a relaxed structure and you can dedicate more time to the game, Double Trouble or Dice Santa are good options. These variants add elements that boost interaction and humor, allowing participants to enjoy each round and get to know each other better.

5. Gauge the Group's Energy and Interest Level

Each group has a different energy level and interest, which should also factor into your decision:

High-Energy Groups: For energetic, enthusiastic participants, Double Trouble and Dice Santa add more humor and engaging tasks. These variants encourage extra interaction and competition, boosting involvement.

Calmer Groups: For groups that prefer a more low-key experience, Speed Elephant is the best choice. The short decisions and simple rules allow everyone to have fun without needing to dive into more complex challenges.

Summary

Choosing the right White Elephant variant depends on many factors, such as the number of participants, event atmosphere, group preferences, time available, and the energy level of guests. Speed Elephant is perfect for larger groups and more formal gatherings, Double Trouble works well among close friends, and Dice Santa adds randomness and humor for more enthusiastic groups. By matching the variant to the group's unique dynamics, you can ensure everyone enjoys a fun and memorable time.

Chapter 4.1: Classic and Universal Gifts

Classic and universal gifts are a great choice for White Elephant parties, as they work well with any group—regardless of age, interests, or the type of gathering. This section covers gift ideas that are both fun and practical, bringing a smile to recipients and ensuring that everyone finds something enjoyable.

1. Kitchen Gifts and Home Gadgets

Kitchen items and home gadgets are classic choices that are always a hit at White Elephant parties. Choose items that are both fun and useful, giving participants a humorous yet practical gift.

Funny Mugs: Mugs with humorous sayings or graphics, like "Not a Morning Person" or "World's Okayest Employee," make a great gift that brings a smile and is perfect for everyday use.

Themed Kitchen Towels: Small towels with funny phrases or seasonal designs make for a practical, lighthearted gift that can fit into any kitchen.

Ice Cube Molds in Fun Shapes: Ice cube trays that create animal- or character-shaped cubes add a fun twist to drinks, making them ideal for casual gatherings.

Magnetic Coasters or Bottle Openers: Gadgets that attach to the fridge are both practical and always within reach, making them a welcome gift.

2. Office or Remote Work Items

Office or remote work-related gifts are perfect for White Elephant parties with coworkers or friends who spend a lot of time at their desks.

Stress Relief Toys: From classic stress balls to mini "fidget spinners" and figurines for the desk, these gadgets help ease tension during stressful moments.

Animal-Shaped Phone Stand: Not only cute, but also practical—it holds a phone on the desk, making it a great everyday gift.

Desk Organizer: Organizers for office supplies in quirky designs help keep things tidy while adding a bit of fun to the workspace.

Funny Notebooks and Pens: Notebooks with quirky covers like "Secret Plans for World Domination" or "Worst Ideas Ever," and pens shaped like animals or movie characters make everyday note-taking more entertaining.

3. Holiday and Seasonal Decorations

Holiday and seasonal decorations are classic gifts, especially appreciated during the Christmas season, when everyone is eager to decorate their home or office.

Holiday LED Lights: Small, battery-powered lights in various shapes, like stars, trees, or hearts, are great for decorating any space.

Humorous Ornaments: Ornaments or tree decorations with funny graphics or phrases, like "Grinch's Favorite" or "Not an Angel," add a lighthearted touch to the holiday season.

Mini Christmas Trees or Fake Snow: Small desktop trees and spray-on artificial snow bring holiday cheer even to small spaces.

Scented Holiday Candles: Candles with scents like "Gingerbread" or "Cinnamon Apple" are a cozy addition that everyone will love.

4. Funny and Unusual Gifts

Funny gifts are a great choice if you want to make participants laugh and add a lighthearted, humorous vibe to the party. They might not be practical, but they're sure to bring a smile.

Funny Socks: Socks featuring food patterns (like pizza or burgers) or animal motifs make for a humorous yet practical gift.

"Surprise" Mug: A mug that looks ordinary on the outside but has a hidden funny message or image inside, like "You've been poisoned," is perfect for a surprise laugh.

Funny Apron: Aprons with playful sayings, like "Queen of the Kitchen," "Grill Master," or "Recipe for Success," are a hit at any White Elephant party.

Inflatable Drink Helmets: Helmets with drink holders are great for casual gatherings where participants are looking to have a good laugh.

5. Relaxation and Comfort Gifts

Relaxation-themed gifts are universally appreciated and can find fans in any group. They're enjoyable, practical, and give recipients a moment of rest and comfort.

Eye Masks: Cute or funny sleep masks shaped like animals or with messages like "Offline" make for a simple yet useful gift that's great for anyone who values relaxation.

Animal-Shaped Pillows: Small decorative pillows in the form of pandas, foxes, or other animals are both decorative and functional as a neck rest during a quick nap.

Funny Slippers: Slippers shaped like animals, zombie feet, or giant fruits are both cozy and amusing.

Bath Sets: Small sets with bath salts, essential oils, or bath bombs make for a universal gift that offers a moment of relaxation after a long day.

6. Mini-Games and Social Gadgets

Mini-games and social gadgets are a great choice for White Elephant gatherings, especially if the party is casual and guests want to keep the fun going.

Card Games: Classic games like Uno, Cards Against Humanity (for adults), or other mini card games are a fun way to keep the party going after the gift exchange.

Fridge Dart Game: A mini dartboard that attaches to the fridge is perfect for social gaming fans and adds a humorous touch to any kitchen.

Mini-Puzzles: Puzzles with funny images or unusual shapes, like pizza slices, make for a small gift that's perfect for spending time in a fun way.

Drink-Making Kits: Kits containing a jigger, shaker, and other bar accessories are ideal for parties where guests like to mix up their own drinks.

Summary

Classic and universal gifts are a tried-and-true choice for any White Elephant party. They're practical with a sense of humor, ensuring that participants will be happy with whatever they receive. By choosing funny mugs, kitchen accessories, seasonal decorations, or relaxation gadgets, you'll add a positive vibe to the party and ensure everyone has a great time.

Chapter 4.2: DIY Gifts

DIY (Do-It-Yourself) gifts add a personal touch to any White Elephant party. These gifts are not only original and often more affordable, but they also show that someone invested time and creativity into making them. With simple DIY projects, you can create gifts that will either amuse participants or have practical use. This section offers DIY gift ideas that are sure to delight your guests.

1. Jars with Homemade Snack Mixes

Jars filled with pre-mixed ingredients make for an easy, enjoyable DIY gift that everyone can appreciate. You can prepare mixes for cookies, brownies, hot chocolate, or tea.

Hot Chocolate Mix Jar: Fill a jar with cocoa powder, sugar, dry milk, then top it with mini marshmallows and chocolate shavings. Tie it with a ribbon and include instructions for making hot chocolate.

Cookie Mix Jar: Layer ingredients for cookies—flour, sugar, chocolate chips, and nuts—in a jar. Attach a label with a recipe so the recipient can easily whip up a treat.

Tea Blend Jar: Fill a jar with a variety of teas, dried fruit, and spices like cinnamon, star anise, or ginger. Add a small tea strainer as a thoughtful extra.

2. Homemade Scented Candles

DIY candles make a practical and aesthetically pleasing gift. Homemade candles are easy to customize with different scents, colors, and decorations.

Soy Candle with Natural Scent: Soy wax candles are simple to make, and you can add essential oils with scents like lavender, vanilla, cinnamon, or orange. Pour the melted wax into small glass jars, add a wick, and let it set.

Candle with Dried Flowers: Choose flowers, such as lavender, roses, or jasmine petals, that can be embedded in wax for a beautiful look and subtle scent.

Coffee Candle: Add coffee beans to the wax to create a candle that not only smells great but also looks appealing. This is perfect for kitchens or offices.

3. Jar of "Good Vibes" Coupons

A jar filled with coupons or challenges is a fun and unique gift that adds positivity and humor.

Challenge Coupons: Fill a jar with small challenges, such as "Smile at three people today," "Give a small gift to someone," or "Say something nice to the person on your left." These can be drawn daily or on special occasions.

Acts of Kindness Coupons: Create coupons with simple acts of kindness like "Invite someone for coffee," "Help someone in need," or "Do something good for yourself." It's a great way to encourage small acts of kindness.

Humorous Challenges: Make a jar with funny challenges like "Tell a joke," "Dance without music for 10 seconds," or "Pretend to be a superhero for 5 minutes." These are great for social gatherings and bring out laughs.

4. DIY Relaxation Kit

Relaxation kits make a universally appreciated gift that everyone will enjoy. You can create small, visually appealing sets with natural ingredients to help the recipient unwind.

Bath Kit: Fill a small jar with Epsom salts, dried lavender flowers, and a few drops of lavender or eucalyptus essential oil. You can also include a few bath bombs or handmade soaps.

Homemade Body Scrub: In a jar, combine brown sugar or sea salt with coconut oil or olive oil. Add a few drops of essential oils, like lemon or peppermint, for a refreshing scent.

Eye Pillow: Fill a fabric sachet with rice or flaxseed, add dried lavender flowers, and sew it closed. This pillow is great for relaxation and can be gently warmed in the microwave for added comfort.

5. DIY Funny Mugs or Glasses

Customized mugs or glasses are a fun DIY gift that you can tailor to the recipient's personality. All you need are mugs or glasses and ceramic markers.

Mug with a Message: Choose a funny phrase or drawing and write it on the mug with a ceramic marker, e.g., "Not a Morning Person," "World's Best Procrastinator," or "Coffee First, Talk Later." Bake the mug to set the design.

Wine Glass with a Funny Saying: On a wine glass, write phrases like "Wine Not?", "If it's Monday, there's no wine," or "Drink responsibly – don't spill." This is sure to please any wine lover.

Glass Decorating Kit: Include a set of glass markers with the gift, along with instructions inviting the recipient to personalize their own glass. Each person can decorate their glass with their own designs.

6. Jar of Small Successes

A "small successes" jar is a positive and inspiring DIY gift that encourages reflection and gratitude for life's little joys.

Gratitude Jar: Fill the jar with small prompts or inspirations for daily entries of things the recipient is grateful for. Add a label suggesting they jot down something each day that brought them joy or was a success.

Jar of Positive Thoughts: Include small slips of paper with inspiring quotes or motivational sayings like "You got this!" or "Take it one day at a time." One slip can be drawn daily to start the day with a positive mindset.

Jar of Small Challenges: Add slips with everyday challenges, like "Call a loved one," "Read a chapter of a book," or "Spend 10 minutes in silence." This is a great gift for people who enjoy trying new things.

Summary

DIY gifts are not only unique but also add a personal charm that makes them stand out at any White Elephant party. With ideas like jars of mixes, homemade candles, personalized mugs, or relaxation kits, participants can enjoy a thoughtful gift that brings a smile and is fully customized. These kinds of gifts are attractive and considerate, making sure there's something for everyone to appreciate.

Chapter 4.3: Gifts for Adults

Gifts for adults at a White Elephant party offer a chance to bring humor, and sometimes a bit of surprise, to the event. These gifts can be both practical and funny, ensuring smiles and a fitting contribution to the adult atmosphere of the gathering. In this section, you'll find gift ideas that will surely delight adult participants—from humorous gadgets and practical items to "sparkling" accessories that add a touch of fun to everyday life.

1. Fun and Creative Gadgets

Humorous gifts are perfect when you want to create a light, playful vibe and get participants laughing. Here are some fun gadget ideas for adults:

Mug with a "Hidden Message": At first glance, the mug looks ordinary, but once it's emptied, a hidden message appears at the bottom, such as "This is just coffee… or is it?", "You've been poisoned," or "Oops!" Perfect for the office or morning coffee.

Stress Toys for Adults: Funny stress balls shaped like unusual objects, such as pizza slices, beer bottles, or silly faces, make great desk accessories and help lighten the mood at work.

Wine Glass with Pour Markers: Glasses with measurement lines labeled "Happy," "Happier," and "Happiest" add humor to evening wine sessions and bring a smile to any gathering.

Miniature Drinking Games: Small game sets, like mini roulette or card games with challenges, are great for parties. They add humor and are a fun way to encourage interaction in a laid-back atmosphere.

2. Practical Gifts with Humor

Practical yet humorous gifts strike the perfect balance between usefulness and fun. Everyone loves a gift that's both functional and makes them smile.

Pillows with Funny Sayings: Pillows with prints like "Nap Queen" or "Master of Naps" are perfect for the couch or bed. They make a comfortable and humorous addition to any room.

Kitchen Towel with a Funny Message: Towels with phrases like "Don't bother, I'm already tired" are a great way to bring some humor into the kitchen.

Mini Emergency Repair Kit: A small toolkit with essentials like a screwdriver, mini wrenches, and duct tape in a compact version—perfect for "emergencies" around the house. A great gift for DIY enthusiasts or fans of practical gadgets.

Funny Kitchen Apron: Aprons with slogans like "Grill Master," "Queen of the Kitchen," or "Caution: I'm Cooking!" make fantastic gifts for those who spend time in the kitchen.

3. "Sparkling" and Unusual Gifts

Some gifts for adults are meant to add a little sparkle to everyday routines. These types of gifts work well at a White Elephant party, especially for participants who appreciate humor and enjoy a touch of luxury.

Mini Bartender Set: A set that includes a shaker, jigger, and strainer makes an ideal gift for those who enjoy experimenting with cocktails.

Elegant Glassware or Mugs: Unique glasses or mugs shaped like skulls, animals, or with a copper finish add sophistication to any gathering and make for an original gift.

Poster with a Funny Motto: Posters with humorous phrases like "Save Water, Drink Champagne" or "Home Office, Sweet Home Office" make a fun addition to home decor, adding character to any space.

Small Desk Decorations: Mini figures of flamingos, cacti, or reindeer add charm and a festive touch to desks or homes, making them great decorative gifts.

4. Relaxation and Wellness Gadgets

Relaxation-themed gifts are a great choice for White Elephant, especially when you want to give something that encourages the recipient to unwind and escape daily stress.

Heated Pillow: A small heated pillow in the shape of an animal or a classic relaxation pillow is perfect for cozy winter evenings and provides comfort after a long day.

Aromatherapy Set: Small sets containing essential oils and a mini diffuser make for a thoughtful gift that helps create a calming environment with pleasant scents.

Eye Mask with a Message: An eye mask with phrases like "Offline," "Beauty Sleep," or "Do Not Disturb" is a practical and funny accessory, ideal for a quick nap at work or relaxation at home.

Bath Set: A small bath set with bath bombs, salts, and a sponge creates a soothing, relaxing bath experience. A perfect gift for anyone who enjoys a home spa day.

5. Social Games and Accessories for Adults

Social games make great gifts for parties, especially if you want participants to enjoy them right away. These gifts bring a fun, relaxed vibe and ensure everyone stays engaged.

Adult Card Games: Card games like Cards Against Humanity or Exploding Kittens are a great way to entertain adults and add humor to any party.

Mini Dart Set: A portable dart game that can be hung on the wall or placed on a table is a fun way to bring interaction and entertainment to a gathering.

Dice Game with Challenges: A small game where the roll of the dice determines fun challenges—ranging from silly tasks to taking a sip of a favorite drink or doing a short dance. It's a great way to get people involved and laughing.

Shot Glass Roulette: A mini roulette set with shot glasses is a fun drinking game that adds a playful touch to the party. It's sure to please anyone who enjoys a bit of risk-taking.

Summary

Gifts for adults at a White Elephant party help create a relaxed, fun atmosphere that livens up any event. By choosing funny gadgets, practical yet humorous items, or relaxation accessories, you ensure that each guest will find something that makes them laugh or is useful in their daily life. Well-chosen gifts add positive energy to the entire gathering and ensure the White Elephant party will be remembered with smiles for a long time.

Chapter 4.4: Themed Gifts

Themed gifts are a great way to give your White Elephant party a cohesive and unique character. You can tailor gifts to a specific theme, such as holidays, movies, summer, or even hobbies that your guests share. In this section, you'll find ideas for themed gifts that bring an original touch to your White Elephant party and help participants embrace the atmosphere of the event.

1. Holiday-Themed Gifts

Holiday-themed gifts are perfect for White Elephant parties held during the Christmas season. They create a festive atmosphere and bring the seasonal joy to life.

Holiday Sweaters or Hats: Funny sweaters with reindeer, Santa, or snowflake designs, or hats with reindeer antlers, are great choices for spreading holiday cheer and adding a festive vibe.

Holiday Mug: A mug featuring Santa, reindeer, or snowflakes is both practical and seasonal, perfect for winter drinks.

Holiday Socks: Socks with Christmas themes like trees, lights, or snowmen are a cozy and fun gift idea.

Gingerbread or Cinnamon Scented Candle: A holiday-scented candle adds warmth and a festive aroma to any room, making it a welcome addition during winter.

2. Movie and Pop Culture Gifts

Movie and pop culture-themed gifts are ideal for cinema enthusiasts and entertainment fans. Participants will appreciate gifts that reference their favorite shows and movies.

T-Shirt with an Iconic Quote: A shirt featuring a famous movie or TV show quote, like "I'll be back" from The Terminator or "How you doin'?" from Friends, is a perfect gift for pop culture lovers.

Mug with a Movie Character: Mugs featuring popular characters like Darth Vader, Harry Potter, or Batman make a great gift for film fans and add a touch of style to their coffee routine.

Collectible Figurines: Mini figurines of famous characters from Star Wars, Game of Thrones, or Stranger Things are a special gift for collectors.

Movie Poster: Posters inspired by classic movies or shows, like a retro Pulp Fiction or Jurassic Park print, make for unique room decor.

3. Vacation and Summer Gifts

Vacation-themed gifts bring memories of summer fun and relaxation, adding a touch of sun and beach vibes to winter gatherings.

Beach Towel with Tropical Print: A vibrant towel featuring palm trees, flamingos, or seashells is a great gift to spark memories of summer holidays.

Thermal Mug or Water Bottle: A colorful thermos or water bottle with a summer theme, like pineapples or palm leaves, is useful both at the beach and on the go.

Flip Flops or Sandals with Prints: Flip flops with tropical designs like hibiscus flowers or smiling suns make for a playful and practical gift that brings a summery vibe.

Mini Drink Umbrellas and Accessories Set: Small umbrellas, palm picks, and colorful straws are a fun way to introduce a beachy vibe to winter gatherings.

4. Book and Literature Gifts

For literature lovers, book-themed gifts are always a hit. These gifts are perfect for intimate gatherings with friends or book club members.

Funny Bookmark: Bookmarks in unique shapes, like a cat, coffee cup, or literary character, are great for any bookworm.

"Old Book" Scented Candle: Scented candles inspired by the aroma of old books or libraries are ideal for people who love being surrounded by books.

Notebook with a Literary Cover: A notebook inspired by classic literature or featuring famous book quotes makes a great gift for those who love reading or writing.

Mug with a Book Quote: A mug featuring a literary quote or classic-inspired graphic, like "I solemnly swear that I am up to no good" from Harry Potter, adds a touch of charm to morning coffee or tea.

5. Eco-Friendly and Natural Gifts

Eco-friendly gifts are an excellent choice for giving something sustainable and functional. These are especially fitting for White Elephant parties among eco-conscious friends and nature lovers.

Reusable Cotton Tote Bags: Reusable shopping bags with fun or inspirational slogans are a practical gift that's perfect for everyday errands.

Metal Straw Set: A set of metal straws in a travel case is a useful, eco-friendly gift—ideal for those who aim to reduce plastic use.

Zero Waste Cosmetic Kit: A small kit with items like soap bars, shampoo bars, and bamboo toothbrushes makes an eco-conscious gift for fans of natural skincare.

Soy Candle: A candle made from natural ingredients like soy wax and essential oils is a cozy, eco-friendly gift for evenings at home.

6. Hobby-Related Gifts

Gifts tailored to the hobbies of participants show that you put thought into your choice. These can relate to sports, crafts, cooking, or other shared interests that bring people together.

Painting or Sketching Kit: A small set with paints, brushes, or pencils is ideal for people who enjoy creating art.

Mini Tool Set: A practical mini tool set for DIY enthusiasts, complete with basics like a screwdriver, tape measure, and small wrenches.

Cookie Baking Kit: Cookie cutters, sprinkles, and a small rolling pin make a wonderful gift for anyone who loves baking and experimenting in the kitchen.

Chess or Card Game Set: A mini set for chess, checkers, or cards is perfect for those who enjoy intellectual games and pastimes.

Summary

Themed gifts allow participants to dive into the chosen vibe of the White Elephant party, enhancing its unique character. By selecting gifts related to summer, literature, pop culture, eco-consciousness, or hobbies, you're introducing more than just items to the party—you're creating shared interests that bring everyone closer together.

Chapter 5.1: Accompanying Mini-Games

Mini-games are a great way to add variety to a White Elephant party, increasing engagement and sparking friendly competition, laughter, and camaraderie. Below are ideas for several mini-games you can weave into your event to make it even more fun and dynamic.

1. Guest Trivia Quiz

A trivia quiz about the guests is a fun way to help everyone learn more about each other and discover funny facts. Preparing a quiz with personal questions adds a unique, friendly touch to the gathering.

How to Play: Before the party, collect fun facts about each guest, such as favorite foods, unusual hobbies, or funny childhood memories. During the event, ask questions and see who knows the group best.

Sample Questions:

- "Who here loves horror movies?"

- "Who is the best baker in the group?"

Prize: The person who scores the most points could win a small prize or a special perk in the White Elephant game, like an extra chance to trade gifts.

2. White Elephant Bingo

White Elephant Bingo adds a new twist by swapping traditional bingo numbers for party-related actions and behaviors, like "someone switches a gift" or "someone laughs till they cry."

How to Play: Prepare bingo cards with White Elephant-related scenarios, such as "someone picks the smallest gift," "someone forgets the rules," or "someone laughs uncontrollably." Players mark off actions as they happen during the party.

Sample Bingo Spaces:

- "Someone forgets the gift-stealing rule"

- "Someone rejects a gift"

- "Someone can't stop laughing"

Prize: The first person to get a bingo could win a small prize or a bonus swap opportunity in the game.

3. Target Toss Challenge

Target Toss Challenge is a lighthearted game that adds an element of surprise and laughter as guests perform fun tasks chosen by chance.

How to Play: Set up a target board with sections labeled with different challenges, like "tell a joke," "dance for 10 seconds," or "sing a holiday song." Guests take turns tossing a dart and completing the task they land on.

Sample Challenges:

- "Share your funniest work story"
- "Pretend to be Santa for one minute"
- "Say three nice things about the person to your left"

Prize: Each person who completes a task could win a small prize, like a holiday treat, or an extra chance in the White Elephant game.

4. Holiday Charades

Holiday Charades is a classic game that provides lots of laughter and helps bring everyone together as they guess holiday-themed actions.

How to Play: Prepare slips of paper with holiday-related phrases like "building a snowman," "Santa delivering presents," or "singing carols." Each person acts out a phrase without speaking while others try to guess.

Sample Charade Phrases:

- "Opening presents"
- "Slipping on ice"
- "Singing holiday songs"

Prize: The person who guesses the most correctly could earn an extra gift swap or a small prize.

5. Surprise Raffle

A raffle adds a layer of excitement to the White Elephant game by giving guests a chance to win surprise prizes or perks.

How to Play: Each guest receives a raffle ticket with the chance to win small prizes or special privileges, like "an extra gift trade," "choose the next person to pick a gift," or "an extra turn at the end of the game."

Sample Prizes:

- "Swap your gift with anyone else's"
- "Pick the next person in line"
- "Win a small additional gift"

Prize: The raffle could include small treats, holiday trinkets, or special game privileges.

6. Holiday-Themed Photo Booth

A photo booth is both fun and memorable, allowing guests to capture moments from the party. It's easy to set up with a festive background and holiday props.

How to Play: Set up a background with holiday-themed props, like Santa hats, reindeer antlers, holiday-themed glasses, and mini signboards with sayings like "Ho Ho Ho!" or "Merry & Bright." Guests can take funny photos in holiday attire.

Sample Props:

- Santa hats and reindeer antlers
- Funny holiday-themed glasses
- Holiday-themed signs

Prize: You could offer a prize for the best photo or most creative holiday look. The photos also make for great party memories.

7. "King of the Swaps" Tournament

The "King of the Swaps" tournament adds a competitive twist by awarding a title to the person who makes the most trades during the White Elephant game.

How to Play: Track how many times each participant "steals" gifts throughout the White Elephant game. At the end, crown the person with the most steals as the "King" or "Queen of the Swaps" and give them a special title or small prize.

Prize: The "King/Queen of the Swaps" could receive a small gift or a final turn to trade gifts at the end of the game.

Summary

Mini-games are a fantastic way to add extra entertainment and interaction at a White Elephant party. Quizzes, bingo, target tosses, and photo booths make the event more engaging, allowing everyone to share laughter and enjoy time together. With these mini-games, your party will have a unique and playful atmosphere that guests will remember long after the holidays are over.

Chapter 5.2: Challenges and Tasks for Participants

Adding challenges and tasks to your White Elephant party can make it more interactive and bring a great deal of laughter as guests take on amusing and unusual tasks. Here, you'll find ideas for challenges and tasks that will make your party even more fun and engaging.

1. Holiday Challenge Round

A holiday-themed challenge round is a great way to set the festive mood and bring the group together. These short, fun tasks can add lighthearted humor to the game.

How to Play: Each guest draws a slip with a holiday challenge they must complete before choosing or swapping a gift. The tasks should be lighthearted to encourage everyone to participate.

Sample Challenges:

- "Sing a line from your favorite holiday song."

- "Do a 10-second Santa dance."

- "Pretend to have a conversation with a reindeer."

- "Invite someone to an imaginary holiday date."

Prize: Anyone who completes their task could receive a holiday treat or a small reward, such as an extra opportunity to swap gifts.

2. Holiday "True or False"

This classic "True or False" game adds an element of mystery and is a fun way for participants to learn quirky facts about each other. A holiday-themed version with Christmas-related statements will spark some laughs.

How to Play: Each person draws a card with a holiday-themed fact that may be true or false. The rest of the group guesses if it's true. If they guess correctly, the participant completes a small challenge.

Sample Statements:

- "The term 'White Elephant' originated in Thailand."

- "Santa originally wore a blue suit."

- "The first Christmas tree in Poland appeared in the 19th century."

Prize: Those who guess correctly might win a special prize or get a "voucher" for an extra gift swap.

3. Holiday "Two Lies and a Truth"

In this game, participants share three statements about themselves—two lies and one truth—and others guess which is true. It's a great way to share fun facts and bring in a guessing game.

How to Play: Each participant takes a turn sharing three statements about themselves—two false and one true. The group guesses which statement is true.

Sample Statements:

- "I once dressed as Santa for a company party."

- "I love winter but have never been skiing."

- "I have a collection of holiday socks and buy new ones every year."

Prize: The best guesser could receive a small prize or special "holiday privileges" in the White Elephant game, like an extra gift selection.

4. Improvised Challenges

Improvised challenges require spontaneous performances or speeches, adding a creative twist to the party. These tasks bring humor and give participants a chance to show their playful side.

How to Play: Each participant draws a slip with a quick performance or dialogue task, often with a holiday theme. The group can then rate the performance, adding an extra level of fun.

Sample Challenges:

- "Tell the funniest holiday story you've experienced."

- "Pretend you're an elf and describe the gift you'd make for the person next to you."

- "Create a 30-second rhyme about a reindeer."

Prize: The person with the best performance could win a holiday trinket or a tasty treat.

5. Word-Swap Game

The Word-Swap Game is a humorous language challenge where participants substitute words in well-known holiday sayings or song lyrics, often resulting in hilarious outcomes.

How to Play: Prepare a list of famous holiday songs or phrases, like "Silent Night" or "Let It Snow," and replace some words with mismatched alternatives. Participants must guess the original phrase from the mixed-up version.

Sample Swaps:

- "Silent Duck" (instead of "Silent Night")

- "It's Raining Cheese" (instead of "Let It Snow")

- "Dance, dance until dawn, reindeer with bananas" (a twist on a popular tune)

Prize: The person who guesses the most original titles could earn an extra gift swap or a fun holiday accessory.

6. Who's Who? – Holiday Characters

The "Who's Who?" game assigns each participant a holiday character, creating humorous interactions and helping guests bond as they try to guess each other's identities.

How to Play: Each participant draws a slip with a holiday character or famous holiday figure (like Santa, Rudolph the Reindeer, or the Grinch). They then act or speak in a way that gives clues to their character.

Sample Characters:

- "Santa Claus"

- "An elf who never smiles"

- "Rudolph the Reindeer"

- "The Grinch pretending to be cheerful"

Prize: The person who best portrays their character and gets guessed first could win the title of "Holiday Character King/Queen" and a small prize.

7. Holiday Roulette – Pick a Challenge

Holiday Roulette is a game where guests spin a wheel or draw numbers to randomly select a challenge, adding an element of suspense to the White Elephant game.

How to Play: Set up a wheel with numbers or use a bag with numbered slips that correspond to different tasks on a list. Each participant draws a number and completes the assigned task.

Sample Tasks:

- "Do a holiday dance."

- "Describe your dream holiday in three words."

- "Sing in an elf voice for 10 seconds."

Prize: Those who complete their challenge might earn special privileges in the game, like an extra gift swap or a small holiday prize.

Summary

Challenges and tasks add a level of competition, humor, and bonding to a White Elephant party, creating a lively and fun atmosphere. Games like "True or False," improvised challenges, and holiday roulette let everyone participate actively and enjoy shared laughter, enhancing the overall festive spirit. With a variety of challenges, guests will enjoy both the gifts and the joy of spending time together.

Chapter 5.3: Holiday Quiz Question Set

A holiday quiz is a fantastic way to warm up the atmosphere at a White Elephant party, with questions that cover Christmas, winter themes, and fun seasonal trivia. The quiz lets participants test their holiday knowledge and serves as a lively, engaging activity. Here's a list of question ideas to make your quiz both fun and informative.

1. Classic Christmas Questions

Classic Christmas questions let participants showcase their basic holiday knowledge on Christmas traditions and culture.

Question: In which country did the tradition of decorating Christmas trees begin?

- Answer: Germany.

Question: What is the original title of "The Grinch"?

- Answer: How the Grinch Stole Christmas!

Question: On which day is St. Nicholas Day celebrated?

- Answer: December 6.

Question: According to tradition, what brings good luck if found in Christmas pudding?

- Answer: A coin.

2. Holiday Movies and Songs

Questions on popular holiday movies and songs add nostalgia and fun to the quiz.

Question: What is the name of the main character in Home Alone?

- Answer: Kevin McCallister.

Question: Who sings "Last Christmas"?

- Answer: Wham!

Question: In the movie Elf, what is the main character's favorite syrup flavor?

- Answer: Maple.

Question: In which movie do we hear the famous line, "It's a miracle on 34th Street"?

- **Answer:** Miracle on 34th Street.

3. Holiday Traditions from Around the World

Questions about holiday traditions from different parts of the world make the quiz more interesting and educational.

Question: In which country do people decorate banana trees for Christmas instead of fir trees?

- **Answer:** India.

Question: In which country is it traditional to have KFC for Christmas dinner?

- **Answer:** Japan.

Question: What is thrown into the fireplace in Spain on Christmas Eve to ward off evil spirits?

- **Answer:** Juniper branches.

Question: In which country is Santa known as "Papa Noël"?

- **Answer:** France.

4. Christmas Symbols and Decorations

Questions about Christmas symbols and decorations help bring participants into the festive spirit.

Question: What is the traditional plant under which people are supposed to kiss?

- **Answer:** Mistletoe.

Question: What do the red berries of holly represent?

- **Answer:** The blood of Christ.

Question: What color is traditionally associated with Santa Claus's suit?

- **Answer:** Red.

Question: What were the earliest Christmas tree decorations made from?

- **Answer:** Fruits, nuts, and cookies.

5. Holiday Treats

Questions about traditional holiday dishes and treats add a bit of festive flavor to the quiz.

Question: What is traditionally hidden in Christmas pudding in England?

- **Answer:** A coin.

Question: What cookies are traditionally prepared in the U.S. for Santa Claus?

- **Answer:** Gingerbread cookies and milk.

Question: Which country is known for panettone, a holiday sweet bread?

- **Answer:** Italy.

Question: What drink is traditionally enjoyed during the holidays in Germany?

Answer: Glühwein (mulled wine).

6. Christmas Fun Facts

Unusual holiday facts and trivia can surprise participants and make the quiz even more enjoyable.

Question: What is the name of the "red-nosed reindeer"?

- **Answer:** Rudolph.

Question: Who are Santa's helpers?

- **Answer:** Elves.

Question: How many reindeer pull Santa's sleigh?

- **Answer:** Eight (or nine, if you include Rudolph).

Question: When was Home Alone first aired on television?

- Answer: 1990.

7. Christmas Legends and Characters

Questions about holiday figures and legends are a great way to test how well participants know the magical characters of Christmas.

Question: What is the name of Santa's "evil twin" who punishes naughty children?

- Answer: Krampus.

Question: Who brings gifts to children in Italy on Epiphany?

- Answer: The witch Befana.

Question: Which saint inspired the character of Santa Claus?

- Answer: Saint Nicholas of Myra.

Question: In which Scandinavian legend does Santa ride reindeer to bring gifts to children?

- Answer: Finnish legend (Finland).

Summary

This holiday quiz question set includes questions from a variety of categories, making the quiz dynamic and engaging. Participants can learn new things about holiday traditions, symbols, food, and culture, creating a festive atmosphere and adding entertainment to your White Elephant party.

Chapter 6.2: Worst Gifts and Biggest Flops

Some gifts, though they might seem funny or unique, often end up as the ones no one wants to take home. The worst White Elephant gifts are those that are impractical, too unusual, or simply not well thought out. These can lead to mild disappointment or even amusing situations when participants try to avoid them during exchanges. Here is a list of common White Elephant flops to avoid at your party.

Overly Personal Gifts

Gifts that are too personal—like toiletries, underwear, or other daily items that have a distinctly private nature—often lead to discomfort and are usually among the least popular choices.

Examples: Foot care kits, toothbrushes, deodorants.

Why it's a flop: Such gifts can feel awkward and may make the recipient uncomfortable.

Outdated Electronics

Old electronic gadgets that are outdated or unusable rarely make good gifts and are more likely to cause confusion than excitement.

Examples: Old phones, cassette players, outdated digital cameras.

Why it's a flop: No one wants to take home a device that is essentially useless or obsolete.

Children's Toys at an Adult Party

Gifts that are more suited for children don't usually go over well at adult White Elephant parties, unless they have a humorous twist that appeals to the group.

Examples: Stuffed animals, crayons, small children's puzzles.

Why it's a flop: Most adults aren't interested in toys more appropriate for kids.

Questionable "Gag" Items

Some gag gifts are meant to be funny, but it's easy to go too far and end up with items that are simply strange or unattractive.

Examples: A "weird fish" desk figurine, a plastic pendant shaped like food.

Why it's a flop: Although they might get a laugh, nobody really wants to display these at home or work.

Tacky Decor

Gaudy or quirky decor items rarely find a happy home, as most people prefer tasteful decorations they feel comfortable displaying.

Examples: Pink plastic palm tree, fish-shaped vase, neon-colored ornaments.

Why it's a flop: Such decorations often come across as tacky and are hard to incorporate into most decor styles.

Unusual-Sized or Oddly Shaped Clothing

Clothing is a risky choice, especially when it's not a universal size or shape. Unusual sizes and styles make it even more likely to be left behind.

Examples: Oversized T-shirt with a strange print, giant pants, vintage-style shawl.

Why it's a flop: Such items are rarely a good fit and often remain unused since few will want to wear them.

Low-Quality Beauty Products

Beauty products can be a tricky category, especially when they're low-quality or involve scents and chemicals. Cheap products or ones with unusual scents often go unappreciated.

Examples: Hand paraffin, cheap soap with strong scents, chemical-based peels.

Why it's a flop: These products can cause allergic reactions or simply be unpleasant, making them a poor choice for White Elephant.

Outdated Calendars and Plain Notebooks

Old calendars and plain notebooks are typically regarded as boring gifts, rarely generating much interest among participants.

Examples: Last year's calendar, plain notebook, promotional notepads.

Why it's a flop: These items are too bland to grab attention and lack the fun factor expected at White Elephant parties.

Samples and Mini Products

Mini-sized products or sample items often feel like freebies and aren't seen as real gifts.

Examples: Skincare samples, hotel mini shampoos, travel-size toothpaste.

Why it's a flop: Sample-sized items feel like an afterthought and aren't particularly appreciated, especially at holiday events.

Gifts with Subtle Insults

Gifts that could be interpreted as critical or passive-aggressive should be avoided, as they may create awkward moments or offend the recipient.

Examples: "How to Lose Weight in 30 Days" book, deodorant, anti-wrinkle cream.

Why it's a flop: Gifts suggesting self-improvement or hinting at personal issues can make the recipient uncomfortable or self-conscious.

Gimmicky or Impractical Items

Items that look useful but end up being impractical are also likely to go unclaimed. People tend to avoid things that will just take up space.

Examples: Banana slicer, mini travel iron, "wet soil" scented candle.

Why it's a flop: These items are either useless or so specific that no one will have a reason to use them.

Promotional or Freebie Items

Promotional gifts or corporate giveaways look cheap and are typically not appreciated as White Elephant gifts.

Examples: Pens with company logos, branded keychains, shopping bags with promotional text.

Why it's a flop: Freebies give the impression of minimal effort, often landing them at the bottom of the popularity list.

Summary

The worst White Elephant gifts are those that are impractical, overly personal, outdated, or look cheap and thoughtless. When choosing a White Elephant gift, aim for something fun and versatile that will appeal to everyone without causing discomfort. That way, the party will be a success, and everyone can enjoy the gift exchange to the fullest.

Chapter 6.3: Most Surprising Gifts

White Elephant gifts are often surprising—sometimes hilariously so, other times simply because of their originality. These gifts stand out, provoke laughter, and sometimes even puzzlement, but they're always memorable for participants. Here are some ideas for the most unusual and surprising gifts that add charm and humor to any gathering.

Office Survival Kit

An office survival kit is a humorous gift that will surely appeal to coworkers and fans of quirky office gadgets.

Sample Contents: Stress ball, mini energy drink, sticky notes, mini coffee shots, snacks, novelty pen.

Why it surprises: It's a playful nod to daily office challenges, filled with handy little items that bring a smile.

Personalized Renaissance-Style Portrait

A portrait or print depicting someone in a classic Renaissance style—say, as a king, queen, or knight—is a unique and amusing yet stylish gift.

Why it surprises: The old-fashioned style combined with personalization is both elegant and hilarious.

Magic Answer Machine

A portable "magic answer" device, like an 8-ball that gives random answers to questions, is an unexpected and fun gift.

Why it surprises: It's a great party game that brings a touch of mystique and humor to any event.

"Weirdest" Kitchen Gadgets Collection

A collection of quirky, little-known kitchen tools that are both practical and a bit absurd—a perfect gift for those who love cooking with a sense of humor.

Example gadgets: Banana slicer, egg separator shaped like a face, spaghetti fork, avocado slicer.

Why it surprises: These items are both functional and funny, adding a unique flair to any kitchen.

Mermaid Tail Blanket

A mermaid tail blanket is a cozy yet whimsical gift, perfect for chilly winter nights.

Why it surprises: The mermaid blanket is not only warm but also a fun, eye-catching accessory that brings joy.

"Spa in a Surprise Egg" Kit

An adult surprise egg filled with spa products—break it open to reveal mini treats for a home spa experience.

Sample Contents: Mini bath bombs, face mask, small lotion, scented candle.

Why it surprises: The act of breaking open the "egg" adds an element of surprise, and the spa products make it relaxing.

Mini Zen Garden for the Desk

A small zen garden with sand, a mini rake, and stones is a gift that brings a bit of calm to the desk space.

Why it surprises: It's a unique decorative item that's also soothing and practical for the office.

DIY Dino Terrarium Kit

A DIY kit for creating a terrarium with a toy dinosaur, plants, and stones is a playful blend of creativity and humor.

Why it surprises: This is a creative DIY gift where participants can add their personal touch, and the dinosaur is an unexpected, funny twist.

"Breakfast Socks" Set

A breakfast-themed sock set printed with images of toast, butter, and eggs—cute and quirky.

Why it surprises: The breakfast socks are an unusual yet cozy accessory that brings smiles with its playful design.

Superhero Apron

A kitchen apron styled after a superhero costume, like Superman, Batman, or Wonder Woman, is both humorous and stylish.

Why it surprises: It makes cooking more fun and gives the wearer a "superpower" in the kitchen.

Origami Kit

An origami kit complete with instructions to make animals, flowers, and other shapes—a gift that requires a bit of creativity and patience.

Why it surprises: Origami is a unique activity that engages participants in a fun and creative pastime.

"Ice Cream Mug"

A mug that resembles a mini-freezer or ice cream container—ideal for ice cream lovers.

Why it surprises: It's a unique and functional mug that any ice cream enthusiast would appreciate.

Mini Holiday Film Projector

A mini projector that can be connected to a phone to project holiday movies on a wall or ceiling—a unique gift for movie fans.

Why it surprises: This gadget creates a mini home theater experience, which is both functional and impressive.

"Countdown to Friday" Clock

A clock or digital timer that counts down to Friday, bringing a touch of humor to the workspace.

Why it surprises: It's a lighthearted gift that boosts the mood by counting down to the weekend—perfect for the office.

"Book of Bizarre Facts"

A book filled with surprising and quirky facts about history, science, or pop culture—a gift that's both fun and fascinating.

Why it surprises: It's the perfect read for winter nights, providing entertainment and unique information.

Summary

The most surprising White Elephant gifts combine humor, creativity, and functionality. From mini projectors and zen gardens to superhero aprons and whimsical mugs, these presents bring personality and memorable fun to the gift exchange. By choosing inventive and amusing gifts, you'll add a unique, playful vibe to your White Elephant party, creating an experience that guests will remember with a smile.

Chapter 7.1: Funny Stories and Anecdotes from Gift Exchanges

White Elephant parties are often filled with laughter and unexpected twists. The surprising gifts, humorous mishaps, and participants' reactions create unforgettable moments that make for great stories. Here are some funny anecdotes and stories that show how a gift exchange can lead to truly entertaining situations.

The "Hidden Treasure" in the Gift Box

At one White Elephant party, a participant picked a beautifully wrapped but suspiciously light package. Upon opening it, they found a single mismatched sock! Initially thought to be a random gag gift, it turned out to have a note at the bottom: "Congratulations! You've earned a free extra swap!" The sock became one of the most frequently swapped items of the night, to everyone's delight.

The "All-Occasion" Scarf

At a company party, someone brought an incredibly long scarf with an odd mix of patterns that quickly earned the nickname "The All-Occasion Scarf." It featured holiday designs, Halloween motifs, hearts, and even patriotic themes. People tried it on for various "occasions," finding it surprisingly warm, and it ultimately became the crowd favorite of the night.

The "Never-Ending Gift" Box

Another event featured a "magic gift box" with seven layers of wrapping paper. Each time someone unwrapped a layer, they found... another box. After all the layers were removed, the final reveal was a tiny bell labeled "Ring for Luck." The humor of the prolonged unwrapping and the eventual reward kept everyone laughing, and the bell turned into the party's good-luck charm.

The Unexpected "Toaster of the Year

One of the most unusual gifts turned out to be... an old toaster. Brought as a joke from home, it sparked interest because of its backstory—dubbed "indispensable for breakfast" but "slightly charred on one side." The participants joked about who would dare to take it, but it ultimately found a surprising fan—a colleague who confessed they'd been looking for that exact model due to its unique "crusty toast" capability!

On-the-Go Breakfast Kit

A mini sandwich toaster, a small jar of instant coffee, and a mug that read, "Ready for Anything!" turned out to be one of the most popular gifts. Although the toaster was a bit worn, it worked, and the mug became an instant hit. The set went home with a colleague who claimed she'd be putting it to good use at the office, to everyone's amusement.

The Gigantic "All-Occasion Sock Collection"

At one event, someone brought a massive box filled with socks featuring all kinds of designs—from holiday themes and unicorns to Hawaiian patterns. Each participant had to draw one pair, leading to laughs as people tried to guess what kind of socks they'd end up with. In the end, everyone was wearing mismatched socks, adding a unique twist to the party atmosphere.

"Who Wants to Be the Zen Master?"

Another party featured a "Zen Master Set"—a mini sand garden with tiny rakes and a booklet titled "Achieve Zen in 5 Minutes." The set went to the person most stressed before the gathering, turning it into an inside joke. The mini garden became a hilarious focal point as the new "Zen Master" carefully raked the sand, drawing laughter from everyone.

The "Superpower Mug" Duel

One of the most "stolen" gifts of the night turned out to be a simple mug labeled "Superpower Mug," allegedly giving "magical" powers when filled with coffee. The mug's appeal led to a playful "duel" between two attendees who were convinced it would bring them luck at work. Finally, it went to the person who came up with the funniest reason for why they needed superpowers.

The "Unique Fridge Magnet Collection"

Someone brought a set of fridge magnets, each with a funny phrase or image, like "Don't Approach Without Coffee" and "Master Chef of the Universe." The magnets became the subject of jokes throughout the night, with people swapping and trading to create the funniest combinations for their "fridges."

The "Alien Encounter" Blanket

An unexpected hit turned out to be a blanket printed with a UFO scene. The blanket was exceptionally cozy, and its alien print quickly became a humorous topic about "unexpected nighttime visitors." The blanket made the rounds, with each new owner pretending they were sleeping "under alien protection."

Summary

These stories show just how funny and unpredictable a White Elephant gift exchange can be. From quirky kits and unusual mugs to sock collections and an alien blanket, the participants enjoyed themselves immensely, and the humorous anecdotes are sure to be remembered for a long time. Thanks to surprising sets, mismatched gifts, and lots of laughter, every White Elephant party becomes a unique experience filled with unexpected twists and shared joy.

Chapter 7.2: The Most Memorable White Elephant Gifts

Every White Elephant party has its standout gifts—those that leave a lasting impression on participants because they're so funny, unique, or unexpected that everyone remembers them for years to come. Here's a list of the most memorable gifts that sparked laughter, awe, or simply stood out in every way.

The "True Detective Adventure" Kit

One participant brought a detective kit complete with a notepad, mini magnifying glass, Sherlock Holmes-style glasses, and even a fake mustache. The party soon turned into an impromptu comedy mystery, with guests acting as "detectives" and taking photos in their humorous disguises.

Why it was memorable: The detective kit involved everyone in the fun, turning the party into a playful crime scene with impromptu performances.

The "Rudolph the Reindeer" Costume

One gift included a full Rudolph costume, complete with big antlers, a red nose, and a tail. The lucky recipient wore the costume for the rest of the night, playing the role of "Rudolph" and keeping everyone laughing.

Why it was memorable: The costume added a festive touch to the event and had everyone laughing, lightening the party's mood.

The "Book of Unusual Questions"

This book was packed with fun, offbeat prompts like, "What would you do if you were president for a day?" or "Name three things you'd change in your daily routine if you could." The gift inspired thought-provoking discussions, as everyone shared their answers and got to know each other better.

Why it was memorable: The question book was a great icebreaker, leading to funny and meaningful conversations that brought the group closer together.

The "Mystical Power Orb"

One gift was a large, colorful orb labeled "Touch to Reveal Your Future." The orb would light up and play sounds at random, creating a mysterious atmosphere. Each guest took turns asking it questions and awaiting their "magical" answers.

Why it was memorable: The orb captivated everyone's attention, as they took turns "foretelling" their futures, adding a playful twist to the party.

Mini Popcorn Machine

Someone brought a small popcorn maker, which became an instant hit. The recipient fired it up right away, treating everyone to fresh, warm popcorn as they continued the gift exchange.

Why it was memorable: The popcorn maker was not only a practical gift but also brought an unexpected snack and a shared experience to the evening.

Unicorn Hooded Blanket

A pink unicorn-themed blanket with a hood, complete with a colorful mane and horn, was an instant favorite. The recipient immediately donned the hood, becoming the "party unicorn" to everyone's delight.

Why it was memorable: The unicorn blanket was both cozy and hilarious, and everyone wanted a chance to try it on and snap photos.

"Survival Kit for the New Year"

One gift was a humor-filled "survival kit" for the coming year, with a mini wine bottle, instant coffee, an eye mask, a "Plan B" pen, and a small notepad titled "Better Days Notebook."

Why it was memorable: This gift was a funny take on the idea of preparing for the unknown, and it resonated with everyone, creating a lasting memory.

Color-Changing Mug

At one party, a color-changing mug that revealed a funny image or saying when filled with hot liquid captured everyone's attention. Guests kept filling it up just to see the "magic" transformation.

Why it was memorable: The mug added a bit of "magic" to the night, and everyone was eager to see the image change with hot coffee or tea.

Mini Tabletop Pool Table

A tiny pool table delighted guests, as they could jump right into a game on the spot. It sparked friendly competition and provided hours of entertainment.

Why it was memorable: The mini pool table was both unique and interactive, keeping the party energized and full of laughter.

"Funny Socks for Every Day of the Week" Collection

One gift was a box set of socks with humorous designs, with a pair for each day of the week, such as "Monday Blues," "Wednesday Win," and "Weekend Joy."

Why it was memorable: The socks entertained everyone, and guests had fun vying for the pairs that matched their personalities best.

"Mystery DIY Set"

This DIY box contained everything needed to make a holiday decoration, including mini Christmas trees, LED lights, artificial snow, and a tiny reindeer. Guests could design their own creations, letting their imaginations run wild.

Why it was memorable: The DIY set allowed everyone to unleash their creativity, bringing a festive touch to the party and resulting in unique decorations.

"101 Fun Holiday Recipes" Book

A cookbook filled with quirky holiday recipes like "Reindeer Pudding" and "Crispy Elf Delight" added humor to the gathering, with some guests even planning to try a few recipes on the spot.

Why it was memorable: The fun recipes added a touch of holiday cheer, and guests were eager to test them out at their own celebrations.

Summary

The most memorable White Elephant gifts combine humor, practicality, and creativity. Each of these gifts was not only unique but brought a special surprise, a chance for shared laughter, or a touch of entertainment for the rest of the evening. In addition to a fun gift, each participant walked away with cherished memories that would bring smiles for a long time to come.

Chapter 7.3: Blunders That Teach (and Amuse)

White Elephant parties are often full of surprises and unexpected twists, with some situations ending in memorable blunders that guests laugh about for years. These funny "lessons" are useful—not only can they help avoid future gaffes, but they also add an element of humor everyone can enjoy. Here are a few of the funniest stories of White Elephant blunders that both entertain and serve as helpful reminders for planning future gift exchanges.

The "Sweet" Box of Disappointment

One participant brought a beautifully wrapped box that seemed packed with candy—a perfect gift for any sweet tooth. However, upon opening, it turned out there was only a single tiny candy inside! The reveal brought both laughs and surprise from the person who picked it.

Lesson: Make sure the gift's contents match its packaging, and avoid overly "symbolic" quantities. Otherwise, it may come across as a prank that isn't always well-received.

The "Luxurious" Hand Paraffin Wax

One attendee gave a well-wrapped hand paraffin wax kit, but unfortunately, the fragrance was incredibly strong and… not very pleasant. Despite the thoughtful intention, the gift quickly became the center of jokes, with participants humorously trying to "pass it on."

Lesson: When gifting cosmetics, ensure the scent is neutral or pleasant to avoid becoming a running joke or the "most-swapped" gift of the night.

The Misguided Motivational Poster

At one party, someone brought a motivational poster with an unusual quote: "Never give up... unless you're tired." Intended to be inspiring, the poster instead became a source of humor, with every person who picked it up trying to trade it immediately.

Lesson: Motivational gifts can be great, but make sure the message is uplifting rather than unintentionally funny or discouraging.

"Animal Lover" Mug—Not Quite

A mug featuring an adorable cat and the phrase, "Best Friend of Humanity... Not Coffee," ended up with a participant who wasn't exactly a pet lover. Trying to pass the mug along turned into a game, as everyone insisted it was "for everyone."

Lesson: Personalized gifts related to specific interests may not hit the mark. Opt for designs that are more universal and suitable for all attendees.

The Clock With No Hands

One gift was a stylish clock that looked modern and sleek—except that it had no hands! Intended as an artistic piece, it was more confusing than functional, leaving guests amused but unsure of what to make of it.

Lesson: While aesthetics are important, functionality matters too! Choose gifts that are amusing but also practical for a White Elephant party.

The "Diet Book" Gag

Someone brought a diet book titled Lose Weight Without Sacrifice as a joke, but it ended up sparking mixed reactions. Although it was meant humorously, some guests felt it was a bit too pointed. The book ultimately became the least popular gift at the party.

Lesson: Health or lifestyle-related gifts can be misinterpreted. It's best to avoid gifts that might feel like a suggestion or critique.

The "Vintage" Cutlery Collection

One guest brought what appeared to be a vintage cutlery set. However, the utensils were mismatched, with each fork and knife from different eras and slightly tarnished.

The odd assortment became a source of puzzled laughter.

Lesson: Vintage gifts can be fun, but make sure they're functional and complete; otherwise, they may just come across as worn-out and impractical.

The XXL Holiday Sweater

At one gathering, a guest brought a holiday sweater in an XXL size, despite no one needing that size. Though it was festive and lovely, it went from person to person, as no one could actually wear it, becoming the subject of many jokes.

Lesson: When gifting clothing, stick to more universal sizes or items like scarves or hats that are a one-size-fits-all solution.

Last Year's Calendar

As a joke, someone gifted a calendar from the previous year. The recipient was a bit confused and didn't know what to do with it. Although intended as a prank, the group agreed it was neither useful nor particularly funny.

Lesson: Jokes involving "outdated" items aren't always well-received. Avoid gifts that are impractical or unusable.

The "Unusual Angel" Figurine

One attendee brought an angel figurine with a rather unique face—it looked more like a cartoon character than a traditional angel. While it did bring some laughs, it also made a few people hesitant, as the angel looked more like a Halloween character than a holiday decoration.

Lesson: Decorative gifts should be visually pleasing and festive. Too quirky a choice might leave the wrong impression.

Summary

White Elephant party blunders are a reminder to keep gifts tasteful, practical, and generally appealing. Sometimes overly personal or impractical gifts can lead to mixed reactions, but each mishap is a learning experience for future gift exchanges. By keeping these lessons in mind, you can avoid similar situations at upcoming parties and better cater to participants' tastes, ensuring the event is both enjoyable and full of laughter.

Chapter 8.1: White Elephant Game Cards

White Elephant game cards are a fantastic way to bring an element of surprise and fun to your gift exchange. These cards can add unique rules and twists, creating unexpected turns and lots of laughs among participants. Each card can contain various tasks, privileges, or surprises that players draw before choosing a gift. Here are some examples of cards you can create to elevate the White Elephant experience.

"Swap" Cards

These cards allow participants to swap gifts, adding a competitive and surprising element to the game.

Sample cards:

- "Swap your gift with anyone of your choice!"

- "Trade gifts with the person on your left."

- "Give your gift to the person who picked right before you."

- "Hand over your gift to anyone in exchange for theirs."

"Block" Cards

Block cards let players protect their gifts from being stolen for one round, introducing a strategic angle to the game.

Sample cards:

- "Block! No one can steal your gift until the end of this round."

- "Protect any gift from being swapped this round."

- "Your next selection is safe from theft! The gift you pick next is protected."

"Extra Pick" Cards

These cards allow players to pick an additional gift, adding a fun twist of luck and surprise.

Sample cards:

- "Pick an extra gift and decide if you want to keep it or pass it on to someone else."

- "You get another pick! If you like it, keep it."

- "Second chance! Open another gift, then decide which one to keep."

"Return Gift" Cards

Return cards let participants put back a gift and try their luck with a new one, often leading to hilarious moments.

Sample cards:

- "Return your gift and pick a new one."

- "Go back to your previous gift if you want—choose again!"

- "Place your current gift back in the pile and select a new one. Good luck!"

"Switch Places" Cards

Switch place cards let players move spots in the picking order, possibly improving their chances of grabbing a popular gift.

Sample cards:

- "Move two places forward in the line!"

- "Switch spots with the person on your right."

- "Trade places with the last person who picked a gift."

"Task" Cards

These cards add interaction and humor, as participants must complete a task before swapping or selecting a new gift.

Sample cards:

- "Sing a holiday song before picking a gift."
- "Tell a joke before making an exchange."
- "Pretend to be Santa Claus for 30 seconds before trading a gift."
- "Pick a gift, but only use one hand!"

"Lucky" and "Unlucky" Cards

Adding lucky and unlucky cards makes the game more unpredictable, as the lucky ones get extra perks while the unlucky ones face funny consequences.

Sample lucky cards:

- "Lucky you! Keep your gift and pick another from the pile."
- "It's your lucky day! No one can take your gift until the end of the game."

Sample unlucky cards:

- "Uh-oh! You have to give your gift to the person on your left."
- "Oops! Trade your gift with someone else, but you can't keep it."

"Protection" Cards

Protection cards allow players to safeguard against certain consequences or other cards, adding an element of strategy.

Sample cards:

- "Protection Card! Use this to guard your gift from being stolen anytime."
- "Protected from 'unlucky' cards! Use it when needed."
- "Keep your gift safe from swaps—no one can take it from you."

"Group Challenge" Cards

These cards encourage group participation in mini-games or group challenges before proceeding with gift selections.

Sample cards:

• "Group Challenge! Play rock-paper-scissors—the winner picks any gift."

• "All players must perform a holiday dance—the best dancer gets to keep their current gift."

• "Group challenge—guess which gift has been swapped the most. Correct guesses earn a prize!"

Summary

White Elephant game cards are an excellent way to add variety, unpredictability, competition, and laughter to the party. They give each participant a chance to shift their position, earn extra perks, or complete fun challenges, making the game even more exciting for everyone.

Chapter 8.2: White Elephant Wish List Templates

Wish lists can make gift selection easier and ensure that everyone finds something delightful. White Elephant wish list templates help participants brainstorm fun, practical, or quirky gift ideas that match the theme of the exchange. Participants can use these ready-made templates, adapting them to personal preferences, making shopping easier and adding to the holiday spirit of the event. Here are some templates to inspire your White Elephant wish lists.

"Funny and Creative Gifts" Template

This template is for humorous gifts that add a playful vibe to the game. These presents are quirky, unexpected, and bound to make people laugh.

Sample ideas:

• A mug with a funny slogan ("Coffee is My Superpower")

• Socks with unique patterns (like cats, pizza, or dinosaurs)

• A book of fun facts ("101 Weirdest Things You Never Knew")

• A superhero apron or a kitchen apron with a humorous theme

- A retro-style drawing kit (colored pencils and adult coloring pages)

"Practical and Useful Gifts" Template

This template is for those who prefer practical gifts that can be used daily, bringing a little joy and utility to everyday life.

Sample ideas:

- A cozy blanket with sleeves for chilly nights
- Relaxation set: mini heated pillow and a calming scented candle
- Insulated bottle or travel mug
- Desk organizer or planner for the upcoming year
- Phone stand or mini tripod for smartphones

"Holiday and Seasonal Gifts" Template

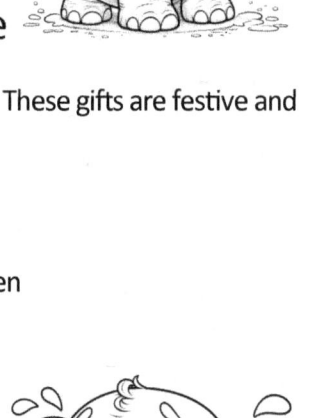

Perfect for anyone wanting to share something seasonal. These gifts are festive and bring out the holiday cheer.

Sample ideas:

- Holiday socks with reindeer, Christmas trees, or snowmen
- A small holiday ornament (like a hand-painted bauble)
- Advent calendar with little surprises
- Scented candle with gingerbread or cinnamon fragrance
- A holiday-themed tea or hot chocolate set

"DIY and Crafty Gifts" Template

For fans of handmade items, this template offers ideas for DIY gifts that come with a touch of personal character and creativity.

Sample ideas:

- DIY soap or candle-making kit
- A jar with cookie mix (layered dry ingredients for chocolate chip cookies)
- Mini herb garden kit with pot and seeds (like basil or mint)
- Holiday ornament-making kit (with glue, glitter, and tiny decorations)
- DIY relaxation set (a small jar of tea, a candle, and an eye mask)

"Unpredictable and Surprise Gifts" Template

This template is ideal for anyone who loves a surprise and wants to add a bit of mystery to the exchange.

Sample ideas:

- "Mystery Box" – a wrapped gift with no hints as to what's inside
- A Magic 8-Ball with funny responses
- Jar full of fun challenges or goals for the new year
- Random mini gadget collection (like a mini flashlight, tiny notepad, and keychain)
- Beginner's tarot or fortune-telling kit

"For Game and Entertainment Lovers" Template

For those who enjoy games and social interaction, this template offers ideas for entertainment-themed gifts.

Sample ideas:

- Deck of Uno or another mini card game
- Pocket-sized board game (like a compact version of a classic game)
- Small dice game set with instructions for fun variations
- Mini tabletop billiards or a small dexterity game

- Trivia quiz set (e.g., a booklet with fun questions)

"Eco-Friendly and Zero Waste" Template

This template is for those who value environmentally friendly and sustainable gift options.

Sample ideas:

- Reusable shopping bag with a funny print
- Set of metal straws with a carrying case
- Zero-waste personal care kit (like bar shampoo and natural soap)
- Water bottle with a filter or recycled travel mug
- Set of wooden travel utensils in a cotton pouch

"Silly and Novelty Gifts" Template

This template includes ideas for quirky, amusing gifts that bring an element of silliness to the exchange.

Sample ideas:

- A book of "fun facts you'll never use"
- A unique kitchen gadget like a banana peeler
- Mug with a surprise message at the bottom ("End of Coffee, End of Hope")
- Fridge magnet with a funny quote ("Secret Food Stash Here")
- Portable laugh track button for instant laughter on demand

Summary

White Elephant wish lists in the form of ready-made templates make it easy for participants to select gifts that fit the theme and bring joy to everyone involved. Whether looking for something funny, practical, eco-friendly, or surprising, these templates simplify the selection process and enhance the festive spirit and excitement of the gift exchange.

Chapter 8.3: Task Coupons for White Elephant Drawings

Task coupons add an interactive and humorous twist to a White Elephant exchange. Before selecting or swapping a gift, each participant draws a coupon with a task to complete, bringing laughter and extra energy to the game. Here are some example task coupons to help create unforgettable moments and spice up the exchange!

"Acting Out" Coupons

These tasks lighten the mood and encourage participants to get creative.

Examples:

- "Pretend to be Santa Claus and cheerfully shout, 'Ho, ho, ho!'"

- "For 30 seconds, act like Rudolph the Red-Nosed Reindeer, red nose and all!"

- "Invite someone to join you in an 'impromptu' carol duet—sing a part of your favorite holiday song together."

- "Do a festive dance, shaking your arms as if you're sprinkling snow everywhere."

"Holiday Confessions" Coupons

These tasks add holiday charm and let participants share favorite memories and traditions.

Examples:

- "Share your funniest holiday memory."

- "Tell everyone what you love most about the holidays."

- "If you could change one holiday tradition, what would it be?"

- "Reveal your favorite holiday movie or song."

"Mystery Gift Presenter" Coupons

These tasks involve describing or handing over gifts in unusual ways, adding humor and surprise to the game.

Examples:

- "Become a salesperson and describe your gift as if it's featured in a TV ad."
- "Present your gift with a dramatic bow, like a professional gift presenter."
- "Come up with three funny uses for your gift."
- "Pretend to 'wrap' the gift with imaginary details, explaining why it's so unique."

"Creative Challenge" Coupons

These coupons allow participants to show off their creative side, adding an artistic touch to the exchange.

Examples:

- "Draw a mini Christmas tree on a piece of paper using only one hand."
- "Make up a quick holiday rhyme in 30 seconds."
- "Sing an improvised song about the gift you just picked."
- "Create a funny story about your gift and share it with everyone."

"Skill Challenge" Coupons

Skill challenges add fun and laughter, especially when they involve a bit of coordination.

Examples:

- "Choose a gift using only your elbows."
- "Spin in a circle three times before picking a gift."
- "Hop on one foot as you pick out a present."
- "Answer three holiday trivia questions before selecting your gift."

"Holiday Trivia and Riddles" Coupons

Trivia and riddles bring a playful element to the game and let participants test their holiday knowledge.

Examples:

- "Answer this question: What is a traditional holiday dessert in England?"
- "What is the name of Santa's most famous reindeer?"
- "How many days are there in the '12 Days of Christmas' song?"
- "What's Santa's favorite drink served with cookies?"

"Dare Challenges" Coupons

Dare challenges add a competitive touch, requiring participants to complete mini-tasks before making a swap.

Examples:

- "Challenge! Find someone wearing a holiday color and swap places with them."
- "Ask the person to your left to swap a small item with you."
- "Do 10 squats before exchanging your gift."
- "Pick two people and have them sing a line from their favorite carol together."

"Random Privilege" Coupons

Privilege coupons give participants a small bonus or allow them to skip a task, adding a fun twist.

Examples:

- "Lucky break—you can skip your task and pick a gift right away."
- "Swap gifts with anyone you choose without completing a task."
- "Pick a gift without looking and keep it if you like it."
- "Your next swap is protected—no one can take your gift from you."

"Rhyming Challenges" Coupons

Rhyming tasks are funny and require a bit of quick poetry, adding a lighthearted touch.

Examples:

- "Before picking a gift, create a quick rhyme in just one line!"

- "Come up with a rhyme about your gift and say it aloud—no rhyming, no gift!"

- "Make a short rhyme about the holidays and win your turn at the gift pile."

- "Sing a line with a holiday twist, then pick a gift for your list."

"Random Bonus" Coupons

Additional bonuses give participants a chance at extra rewards or small gifts, boosting the fun even more.

Examples:

- "Bonus! Choose an extra gift for someone else—let them decide if they want to keep it."

- "You're in luck! Skip this task but keep your gift."

- "Random bonus! You can steal any gift from another player."

- "You get a small bonus gift—pick a mini reward from the organizer."

Summary

Task coupons for a White Elephant gift exchange add interactive fun and excitement to the event. With challenges, privileges, and funny tasks, participants get a chance to show off their creativity, test their skills, and share a memorable time in a joyful setting.

Chapter 9.1: Humorous Holiday Wishes

Funny holiday wishes add lightheartedness, joy, and festive spirit to any White Elephant gathering. They're perfect for greeting cards, task coupons, or sending as playful holiday messages to friends and family. Here are some ideas to bring laughter and holiday cheer to everyone!

For the Sweet Tooth

"Wishing you holidays full of cookies, chocolate, and cups of hot cocoa! After all, calories don't count when Santa's around!"

"May your holidays be sweeter than gingerbread—and may you always find room for one more piece of cheesecake!"

With a Wink

- "May your gifts be more on point than my jokes at family dinner!"

- "Here's to no holiday mishaps this year, and may the only surprises be the perfect gifts!"

- "Hope Santa isn't the only one bringing you joy this year... and may all the aunties skip the 'When are you settling down?' questions!"

For the Perpetually Busy

- "May you finally have time to relax this holiday... and may all your gifts wrap themselves!"

- "Here's to more free days on your calendar than meetings—and a shorter line for holiday treats than ever before!"

With a Santa Joke

- "Here's hoping for more gifts than coal this year—remember, Santa sees everything!"

- "May Santa forget all your little 'mishaps' this year and bring you gifts... or at least a great excuse!"

For Holiday Food Lovers

"Wishing you dumplings that taste like Grandma's, endless bowls of soup, and a spot for dessert that never fills up!"

"May your holiday table be overflowing with treats—and your belly with laughter!"

For the Chill Enthusiast

- "May these holidays be as relaxing as a perfect day off… with a side of chocolate and festive movies!"

- "Here's to the break you deserve—may it be long, cozy, and unending!"

For Holiday Movie Fans

"Wishing you holidays like the best holiday movies: a bit of magic, lots of laughs, and a happy ending (aka, a well-rested you)."

"May every holiday day be even better than Home Alone… because we all watch it, but maybe it's time for new adventures?"

For Lovers of Cozy Socks

"May your holidays be as warm as your thickest winter socks and as comforting as a cup of tea on a snowy day."

"Wishing you all the cozy socks you need, and enough holiday cheer to make every day feel like Christmas morning!"

For Family Jokesters

- "Here's to holidays so fun that the whole family laughs—even at your worst jokes."

- "May family gatherings be filled with warmth, laughter, and… a touch of patience for all those family questions!"

With a Wink for New Year's

"May the New Year be better than the one where nothing went right... and here's hoping Santa finally brings you what you really want!"

"Wishing you a New Year full of happiness, laughter, and small miracles (the kind where no one notices you didn't clean up after the holidays)!"

Summary

Humorous holiday wishes are a great way to make time with loved ones or coworkers feel light and joyful. They're easy to customize for friends or family, and bring laughter to holiday moments. With these funny wishes, every moment becomes warmer and full of good cheer!

Chapter 9.2: Humorous Quotes About Gifts and the Holidays

Nothing lightens up the holiday atmosphere like a good sense of humor! Funny quotes about gifts and the holidays bring everyone a dose of joy and a bit of playful spirit to White Elephant exchanges. These humorous quotes are perfect for gift tags, holiday cards, or just to spread some festive cheer. Here are a few funny quotes that are sure to make everyone smile!

On the Challenges of Holiday Gift Shopping

- "Remember, it's the thought that counts... especially if you forgot to buy a gift!"

- "Finding the perfect holiday gift is an art – that's why I always end up with socks."

- "I got you a gift because I know you like me... or because I ran out of time."

- "The perfect gift? One that doesn't need to be returned!"

On Santa and Stocking Stuffers

- "Remember how well-behaved you were this year... and just hope Santa got it wrong!"

- "Not sure if I earned a lump of coal this year, but just in case, I left out cookies and milk."

- "They say Santa watches all year... good thing there's New Year's to start fresh!"

- "I hear Santa brings coal for the naughty – may your gift be just a twig!"

On Holiday Eating

- "Holidays are the one time my healthy eating plans hide in the cookie jar."

- "Here's to your belly growing only from laughter... and maybe a few gingerbread cookies."

- "Holidays: the time when the number of dumplings on your plate doesn't count."

- "Counting calories during the holidays? That's like counting on Santa to take them away."

On Holiday Decorating

- "Holiday decorations: the best excuse to make your house look like a bauble factory."

- "Not sure what shines more during the holidays – the tree or my mood after a fourth cup of mulled wine."

- "Decorating the tree is like gymnastics – you never know if that ornament is hanging straight!"

- "Holidays are the magical time when the house looks like a commercial and everyone pretends it's always like that."

On Family Gatherings

- "Can't decide what's better: seeing family or escaping after Christmas dinner."

- "Holidays – the time we meet up with family to discuss everything we avoid the rest of the year!"

- "Family holidays: the time when you're not sure how much you'll eat or how many times you'll hear, 'So, when's the wedding?'"

- "Nothing like a holiday meal that turns into a talk about the past, the future, and all your life decisions."

On Holiday Relaxation (Or Lack Thereof)

• "Holidays are the time you dream of rest... and get a long to-do list from Santa instead."

• "Adulthood: realizing 'holiday break' means shopping, cooking, and gift-wrapping."

• "Dreaming of a white Christmas... and an extra hour of sleep!"

• "Holidays – the time when cleaning and decorating remind us of everything we still haven't done."

On Holiday Wishes and Expectations

• "Merry Christmas! Here's hoping your gifts are better than my New Year's resolutions."

• "All I want for Christmas is some free time... and maybe a little coffee."

• "Whoever said holidays were relaxing has clearly never shopped for the perfect gift for the in-laws!"

• "May your holidays be filled with love, happiness... and everything you start thinking about back in November."

On Unexpected Gifts

• "Thanks for the gift... even if I'm not quite sure what it is."

• "The perfect gift is one that looks nice... until you open the box."

• "Any gift is a good one – especially if it comes with a gift receipt!"

• "When you open a gift and wonder if you should be happy... or worried."

On Winter Weather and the Holiday Spirit

• "Let it snow... at least on the tree, because the parking lot is just slush at this point."

• "Winter, snow, and carols – the lovely illusion that makes December feel cozy."

• "The holiday magic starts when you realize snowdrifts don't matter because there's warm cocoa inside."

- "Nothing like the sight of the first snow… which turns to slush on my commute."

On New Year's Resolutions

- "My New Year's resolution? To stick with it longer than Christmas dinner lasted!"

- "Don't ask about my New Year's resolutions – I still haven't kept last year's."

- "2024 – I don't know what it'll bring, but maybe I'll start by surviving the holidays."

- "New Year, new resolutions… and the same old problem keeping them!"

Summary

Humorous quotes about gifts and the holidays are a wonderful way to ease into the festive season, add some lightness to holiday gatherings, and keep everyone in a cheerful mood. They're perfect for holiday cards, gift tags, or simply to sprinkle into holiday conversations and bring everyone a touch of holiday joy.

Chapter 9.3: Wishes to Make Guests Laugh

Humorous holiday wishes are a fantastic way to bring lightheartedness and joy to festive gatherings. These wishes can entertain guests, add charm to shared celebrations, and ensure everyone feels the holiday spirit. They're perfect for White Elephant parties, family dinners, or gatherings with friends. Here are some cheerful wishes that are sure to bring smiles and get guests into the holiday spirit.

For Workaholics and Homebodies

- "May this holiday be the only time of year you can guiltlessly relax on the couch and pretend there's nothing on your to-do list!"

- "Wishing you holidays full of sweet laziness, hot cocoa, and movie marathons—because who says the holidays have to be busy?"

- "May your holiday be so long and peaceful that you forget what your inbox and task list look like!"

For Foodies and Sweet Tooths

• "May the dumplings never end, and the soup stay warm—let your stomach be merry all holiday long!"

• "Wishing you a holiday full of treats you've waited all year for… and for the diet to take a backseat until New Year's!"

• "May your holidays be full of calorie-free food and double-desserts!"

For the "Holiday Sleuths" (Those Who Peek at Presents)

• "May the gifts under the tree be so mysterious that you can't guess what they are… unless you find the receipt!"

• "May your holiday intuition be at its peak, and each gift be a pleasant surprise—even if it's another pair of socks!"

• "Wishing you a holiday full of gifts better than last year's… and the thrill of not discovering what you're getting ahead of time!"

For Fans of Holiday Traditions

• "May your home smell of pine, and holiday carols remind you that the best holidays are spent in good spirits and without rush."

• "Wishing you traditions that always work and fresh new ideas to bring laughter to your holidays!"

• "May you enjoy every moment, even if someone sings a carol just a little too loudly!"

For Holiday Decorating Enthusiasts

• "May your holiday decorations be so beautiful that even Santa can't ignore them—and if he spots your house from afar, you might just get an extra gift!"

• "Wishing you a tree that can handle all the ornaments and lights that never go out—even if everything else does."

• "May each ornament find its perfect place, and the holiday spirit stay in your home through January (or longer)!"

With a Wink for Family Gatherings

- "May your family gatherings be full of love, laughter, and… absolutely no questions about your personal life!"

- "Here's to hoping every aunt and uncle skips the 'When's the wedding?' and 'How's work?' questions—because holidays are for relaxing!"

- "May your holidays be warm with family cheer and at a safe distance from topics that might stir things up!"

For Dreamers of a White Christmas

- "May snow fall this holiday season, at least enough to look nice in photos… then melt before it's time to shovel!"

- "Wishing you a white Christmas… even if the only white is the wrapping paper on your presents!"

- "May this year's snow be enough to build a snowman—or at least to keep the street white for a day."

For Fans of Cozy Socks and Christmas Sweaters

- "Wishing you holidays as warm as your thickest Christmas socks and your reindeer sweater you'll definitely only wear once a year!"

- "May your holiday be full of coziness and cheer… and may your reindeer sweater prove you've got plenty of humor!"

- "May your Christmas socks be warm, and your holiday sweater just loose enough to fit all the treats!"

For New Year's Resolution-Makers (With a Sense of Humor)

- "May the New Year bring you everything you want—even if your resolutions only last until February!"

- "May your New Year's resolutions be as optimistic as your gift list—and may they last just a little longer than the holiday decorations!"

• "Wishing you success in every New Year's plan, but if not, at least some good laughs along the way!"

For Those Seeking Relaxation and Calm

• "May these holidays bring you peace that can't be found on any shopping list or fit under any tree."

• "Here's to finding a moment to truly unwind, sip something warm, and enjoy the holidays as you've always wanted."

• "Wishing you true peace and joy this holiday, no matter what surprises the gifts might hold."

Summary

Lighthearted holiday wishes are a perfect way to add cheer and humor to holiday gatherings. With something for everyone—foodies, workaholics, snow lovers, and seekers of peace—these wishes make the holidays feel lighter and help everyone feel joyful, no matter what surprises await under the tree.

Chapter 10.1: Tips for Future Holiday Gatherings

White Elephant parties are all about laughter, surprising gifts, and having a great time. However, they can also be a bit stressful—especially if you're worried about finding the perfect gift or wondering what surprises await in the gift swap lineup. Here are some tips to help you not only survive but thoroughly enjoy your next White Elephant party!

Choose a Gift That's Universal but Fun

It's tough to please everyone, so aim for something that brings a smile and can be useful to anyone.

Tip: Look for gifts that combine humor with practicality, like funny mugs, aprons with quirky sayings, or small gadgets that everyone can enjoy, like festive socks or scented candles.

Avoid Gifts That Are Too Personal

White Elephant gifts should be neutral; overly personal items can make people feel awkward.

Tip: Skip cosmetics, specific-sized clothing, or items that are too individualized. Instead, choose something everyone would be happy to bring home.

Prepare for Laughs and Surprises

Remember, White Elephant is about having fun and not necessarily about finding the perfect gift.

Tip: Be ready for the unexpected! Whatever you end up with, smile and enjoy it as part of the game.

Get Creative—Presentation Counts!

Sometimes, the way you wrap a gift can be just as entertaining as the gift itself.

Tip: Consider using humorous packaging—like a huge box for a small gift or an unusual container (a soda can or a different item's box) to throw others off.

Strategize Your Swap Moves

If you're particularly attached to a gift or eyeing a specific one, pay close attention to the exchange order and the rules of the game.

Tip: Some games allow "locks" or extra exchanges. Swap smartly and keep track of the order to improve your chances of holding onto a favorite item.

Stick to the Budget and Keep It Reasonable

White Elephant parties aren't the place for expensive gifts. Sticking to the budget keeps the game lighthearted and stress-free.

Tip: Choose a gift within the agreed price range. Don't go overboard—remember, the focus is on humor and shared fun, not material value.

Be Prepared for "Gift Hijacks"

A big part of the fun is that gifts often change hands multiple times. Be ready for your chosen item to be taken.

Tip: Approach the game with a relaxed attitude, keeping different outcomes in mind. Even if your chosen gift goes to someone else, remember that the real fun lies in the game's unpredictability.

Embrace the Holiday Spirit and Good Cheer

A White Elephant party is a time to unwind and have fun in a festive atmosphere, so don't take it too seriously.

Tip: Come with a mindset focused on laughter and quality time with family or friends. It's the perfect occasion to celebrate the holidays in a lighthearted, casual setting.

Be Ready for Jokes and a Little Friendly Banter

White Elephant is all about humor and surprises—be ready for funny gifts and friendly teasing.

Tip: If you end up with a silly, strange, or less-than-useful gift, take it in stride and laugh it off. This kind of party is meant for having a good time together, no matter what you find in the box.

Enjoy Every Moment and Make Memories

The best part of White Elephant is the shared laughter and good times with great company.

Tip: Focus on the moments you're sharing—funny swaps, jokes, and surprising gifts. These memories make the holidays even brighter and create lasting holiday joy.

Summary

White Elephant parties are all about kicking back and enjoying the holidays in a relaxed, friendly atmosphere. With these tips, you can approach the next holiday gathering with humor and ease, remembering that the true essence of the game is in the shared laughter and light-hearted fun. So relax, have fun, and may your next White Elephant party be filled with joy, surprises, and memorable gifts!

Chapter 10.2: How to Choose the Perfect White Elephant Gift

Choosing the perfect gift for a White Elephant party can be challenging, as it should be both funny and universally appealing. A well-chosen gift brings laughter, sets a cheerful tone, and makes everyone eager to win it. Here are some tips on how to pick a gift that will win over everyone!

Stick to the Budget

White Elephant is about fun, so gifts don't need to be pricey—what counts is the laughter and the atmosphere, not the value.

Tip: Set a budget (usually $10 to $20) and stick to it. The best gifts are often the simplest and most humorous—creativity matters more than cost.

Choose Something Practical but Funny

Gifts that are useful yet bring a smile are often the biggest hits at White Elephant.

Examples: A mug with a funny saying, a notepad with quirky designs, holiday-themed socks, a silly pillow, or a kitchen apron with "Master Chef" written on it.

Go for Festive-Themed Gadgets

Nothing sets the holiday mood quite like festive-themed gifts—think cozy socks, Christmas mugs, or funny holiday sweaters.

Examples: A snowman-shaped mug, quirky ornaments, a mini gingerbread cookie-making kit, or cinnamon-scented candles.

Funny Games and Gadgets

Small party games or fun gadgets can instantly bring everyone into the fun and get people involved.

Examples: A mini board game, novelty playing cards, a "magic 8-ball" for predictions, a mini tabletop pool game, or a "Truth or Dare" card game.

DIY Gifts for the Creative Types

Handmade gifts or DIY kits are not only creative but also add a personal touch.

Examples: A DIY candle-making kit, a mason jar with cookie mix, a holiday ornament-making kit, or a small kitchen herb garden starter set.

Gifts with a Surprise Element

Gifts that hide a surprise or are wrapped creatively add excitement and make everyone curious.

Examples: A box filled with mini gifts (like candies or fun keychains), a mystery tin, a "golden egg" filled with treats, or a mini-gadget collection with "something for everyone."

Books and Guides with a Humorous Twist

Books filled with funny advice or quirky facts make for a great choice—they're universal and often spark amusing conversations.

Examples: "101 Fun Facts You'll Never Need," "Guide to Hilarious Proverbs," a mini puzzle book, or a funny personality quiz booklet.

Mini "Relaxation" Kits

Spa sets or small relaxation accessories are always appreciated, especially after a long day or the holiday hustle and bustle.

Examples: A mini scented candle, a small bath salt set, an eye mask, or a cozy throw blanket for winter evenings.

Funny Kitchen Accessories

Quirky kitchen gadgets are practical yet fun gifts that often become party favorites.

Examples: A toaster that leaves funny designs on toast, silly cookie cutters, a kitchen apron with a joke, a banana peeler, or a reindeer-shaped salt and pepper shaker.

Always a Hit: Holiday Socks and Sweaters

Festive socks with reindeer or ornaments, or a sweater with a funny holiday theme, are classics that add to the party's holiday spirit and bring smiles.

Examples: Cozy socks with Christmas motifs, funny reindeer sweaters, a Santa hat with a pom-pom, or animal-themed mittens.

Summary

Choosing the perfect White Elephant gift doesn't have to be difficult. The key is finding something that's universal, funny, and within budget. Whether you go for something practical, humorous, holiday-themed, or creative, remember that the main goal is to have fun. Pick a gift that brings a smile, is a little surprising, and will leave everyone at the party with fond memories of a good time together.

Chapter 10.3: Preparing for Surprises and Challenges

White Elephant parties are all about fun, but they're often full of surprises and challenges—especially when funny rules and unpredictable gift exchanges are involved. Being prepared for different scenarios will help you fully enjoy the game without being caught off guard. Here are some tips to keep you ready for whatever your next White Elephant brings!

Keep an Open Mind – Embrace Every Gift with Humor

White Elephant gifts can be surprising, odd, or downright impractical. Accept them with a smile and treat each gift as part of the fun.

Tip: Remember, this isn't just a typical gift exchange—it's a game meant to spark laughter. Whatever lands in your hands, accept it joyfully and add a humorous comment to keep the mood light.

Be Ready for "Thefts" and Quick Exchanges

White Elephant is a game where anyone can lose their newly-won gift to another player. Mentally prepare yourself for your favorite prize to be "stolen."

Tip: Instead of getting attached to a specific item, approach each exchange with flexibility. Sometimes it's even more fun to watch a gift bounce from person to person, and you might end up with something just as exciting in the end.

Get to Know the Game Rules

Every White Elephant event can have unique rules, such as limits on exchanges, "blocks" on gifts, or bonus challenge cards. It's helpful to learn them early on.

Tip: If the host introduces extra rules, like the ability to block a gift after two exchanges, keep that in mind. Understanding the rules will help you navigate the game smoothly and boost your chances of snagging your favorite gift.

Prepare Short Wishes or Jokes for Each Round

Sometimes the game involves giving a short toast or telling a joke. Be ready for this, especially if someone chooses your gift or during each exchange.

Tip: Have a few quick, funny holiday wishes or anecdotes ready—they'll keep everyone entertained and make your turn memorable.

Have a Plan B for Gift Swaps

Sometimes the gift you picked doesn't quite meet your hopes or is frequently "stolen." It helps to keep an eye on other options that might also bring you joy.

Tip: Watch the other gifts as the game unfolds and mentally list a few "backup options." Flexibility is key to making the most of White Elephant!

Be Creative and Ready to Make Quick Decisions

Some White Elephant versions require speedy swaps or timed challenges, adding to the game's energy. Staying ready will help you tackle unexpected situations.

Tip: Don't hesitate to make quick choices and seize opportunities—there are no wrong moves in White Elephant. The most fun happens when everyone dives into exchanges spontaneously.

Prepare for Silly Challenges and Tasks

Organizers often add bonus tasks to the game, like singing a carol before an exchange or doing a silly dance. Be ready for these added challenges.

Tip: Embrace these challenges with humor and an open mind. Even if you have to sing a carol or perform a holiday dance, treat it as a chance to bring extra joy to the gathering.

Bring Small "Exchange" Gadgets

If you think you might end up with a gift you're not thrilled about, bring a few small, funny gadgets to offer in trade with other players.

Tip: Little items like a keychain, mini flashlight, or tiny notebook can come in handy as added exchange tokens or "gag" gifts if an unwanted present comes your way.

Stay Relaxed – It's All About Having Fun

The main goal of a White Elephant party is to laugh and go with the flow. Even if your gift doesn't match your expectations, focus on the festive mood.

Tip: Keep an open and flexible attitude. White Elephant is a game meant for shared laughs, fun, and light-hearted moments, so enjoy each round without taking it too seriously.

Embrace the Unpredictability of the Game

White Elephant parties are full of unexpected twists—that's what makes them special. Sometimes the best gifts are the ones you never saw coming!

Tip: Embrace the spontaneity of the game and enjoy whatever surprises come your way. The laughter and holiday spirit are well worth every surprise.

Summary

White Elephant is a game designed to make everyone laugh and enjoy the festive spirit. Being prepared for surprises and challenges ensures you'll fully enjoy the fun, no matter what gifts come your way. Remember, the goal is all about laughter, a joyful atmosphere, and spending good times with the people you're with.

Summary: White Elephant Book for Adults

White Elephant parties are unique holiday gatherings filled with laughter, surprises, and a growing sense of tradition. This book serves as a comprehensive guide, introducing readers to the ins and outs of organizing and participating in these memorable games. From selecting the perfect gifts to understanding the rules, creating fun challenges, and inspiring out-of-the-box gift ideas, this book goes beyond a simple how-to. It's a collection of ideas designed to spark creativity and enjoyment for hosts and participants alike.

Each chapter provides practical tips paired with humorous touches to help readers approach the game with a light-hearted perspective. Inside, you'll find advice on choosing the ideal gifts, tips for surviving a game filled with "steals" and swaps, and ready-made wish list templates, challenge coupons, holiday quotes, and funny greetings to keep everyone entertained. Additional sections explore creative gift-wrapping ideas, challenges, and surprises that will make the event even more thrilling.

The book reveals that White Elephant parties are more than just a gift exchange—they're a chance to celebrate with loved ones, create memories, and enjoy time together. Each participant gets to experience fun and spontaneity, making the party a perfect occasion for laughter, jokes, and strengthening bonds.

In White Elephant Book for Adults, you'll find everything you need to make your party unforgettable. Whether it's your first time hosting a White Elephant or you're a seasoned pro, this book will help you unlock the full potential of the game, embracing all its surprises with humor and a festive spirit.

Thank you for choosing White Elephant Book for Adults as your guide to holiday fun filled with laughter, surprises, and unforgettable memories. I hope this book has helped you organize a memorable White Elephant party that will bring joy to you and your loved ones.

Each game and gathering is unique, with every participant adding their own special touch. It's your creativity and sense of humor that truly give White Elephant parties their charm. I'm grateful to have been a part of this adventure with you and wish you many laughter-filled moments as you exchange gifts.

It would mean a lot to me if you'd share your experiences and feedback on this book. Your insights will help me understand what you enjoyed and how I can improve in the future. I look forward to hearing your reviews and stories from your parties—every opinion is valuable.

Thank you for bringing the magic of the holidays to life in your gatherings!

www.ingramcontent.com/pod-product-compliance
Lightning Source LLC
LaVergne TN
LVHW010405070526
838199LV00065B/5899